Clay
Water
Brick

Clay
Water
Brick

FINDING INSPIRATION FROM ENTREPRENEURS

WHO DO THE MOST WITH THE LEAST

Jessica Jackley

SPIEGEL & GRAU

NEW YORK

Published in the United States by Spiegel & Grau, an imprint of Random House, a division of Penguin Random House LLC, New York.

Spiegel & Grau and the House colophon are registered trademarks of Penguin Random House LLC.

Library of Congress Cataloging-in-Publication Data

Jackley, Jessica.
Clay water brick : finding inspiration from entrepreneurs who do the most with the least / by Jessica Jackley.
pages cm
ISBN 978-0-679-64376-0
eBook ISBN 978-0-679-64378-4
1. Jackley, Jessica. 2. Businesspeople—Case studies.
3. Entrepreneurship—Case studies. I. Title.
HB615.J27 2015
338'.040922—dc23   2014036552

Printed in the United States of America on acid-free paper

www.spiegelandgrau.com

9 8 7 6 5 4 3 2 1

First Edition

Book design by Caroline Cunningham

For my first investors, Mom and Dad; for my inspiration and partner in all things, Reza; and for our most successful ventures—Cyrus, Jaspar, and Asa. I love you.

AUTHOR'S NOTE

Every entrepreneur's story in this book is portrayed with as much accuracy and detail as my memory, notes, and research provide. In some cases my own firsthand encounters were years ago, and I have lost the last names—and sometimes the first names too—of those individuals along the way. Thus I have been unable to check back with those entrepreneurs for errors or misunderstandings in our conversations (in many cases a translator was present to help with the interviews). In a few cases, I have deliberately changed the names of the entrepreneurs and have omitted or altered other identifying details out of respect for their privacy. For example, this is the case for all Kiva-related entrepreneurs.

It has been my goal and passion over the years to share stories of the entrepreneurs I've met with honesty, integrity, and transparency. This spirit is what inspired Kiva, and reflects my belief that it is everyone's responsibility to represent one another with this kind of intention: to tell one another's stories as they would tell those stories themselves. This is what I have aimed to do in this book.

CONTENTS

FOREWORD

BY JEFFREY D. SACHS

"The world needs you," Jessica Jackley tells her readers. This is true. But it is also true that the world needs Jessica Jackley. She is very special: compassionate, bold, empathetic, ready to learn, and willing to fail, and she possesses the enormous talents necessary to succeed in world-changing ways. The co-founder of Kiva and other innovative endeavors to fight poverty and champion entrepreneurs, Jackley is an inspiration, and her moving account of her lifelong efforts to improve the world will inspire countless others to follow in her path.

Jackley's book is a very special case study—in fact, an autobiographi-cal rumination—on entrepreneurship: her own, plus the inspiring entre-preneurs she has met along the way, from Silicon Valley to impoverished villages of East Africa and beyond. She tells her story and theirs with flair, remarkable honesty, at times piercing humor, and shrewd insights. We are watching a wonderful entrepreneur, and a great storyteller, at work.

JEFFREY D. SACHS is Director of the Earth Institute at Columbia University, Spe-cial Advisor to UN Secretary-General Ban Ki-Moon on the Millennium Develop-ment Goals, and author of *The End of Poverty* (2005) and other works.

For Jackley is forging a path all her own and takes us along on her incredible journey. It is as if we are following the traveler in Robert Frost's great poem, who took the road less traveled by, and that has made all the difference.

As she explains, Jackley was a most unlikely entrepreneur, at least in the conventional sense of the term. She was not a business school hotshot (at least not at first). She was not aiming to make a personal fortune with the latest killer app. She had never run a business. What she did do, however, was listen carefully in Sunday school when she first heard how Jesus called upon his followers to help "the least" among them. And she listened carefully once again when she heard Nobel laureate Muhammad Yunus describe the possibilities of microfinance. Arriving at Stanford University as a young staffer, Jackley combined her deep moral commitments, Yunus's insights, and Silicon Valley's entrepreneurial zest to invent a wholly new force for fighting poverty: crowdsourced microfinance in the now-famous social enterprise, Kiva.

As Jackley makes clear, Kiva was anything but a straight shot to success. Her main point, perhaps, is that entrepreneurship is rarely that way. She and her co-founder invent, test, learn, fail, reinvent, and continue to move forward throughout the early days of Kiva's existence, and she does the same as the next decade of her career unfolds. Jackley seems to embody one of Silicon Valley's most important features: the drive for success coupled with the absence of fear of failure—or at least the ability to keep such fear under wraps. Kiva eventually triumphs, though not without personal and professional costs along the way, all movingly described by Jackley in a way that keeps the reader both riveted and vicariously educated.

As remarkable as Jackley's experiences are the insights she gleans from the wonderful businesswomen and -men she meets and helps along the way. Most are people living in dire rural poverty almost unimaginable in the United States, yet with personal character, drive, and resilience that offer us great inspiration and life lessons. Jackley is inimitable in sharing their experiences with tenderness, concision, and insight: a treasure trove for young entrepreneurs who will be inspired to join the growing legions engaged in ending poverty in our time.

During the past fifteen years, the Millennium Development Goals (MDGs) have been the world's guideposts for fighting poverty. MDG 1 called for poverty in the developing countries to be cut by half between 1990 and 2015. That has happened. The reasons for success are many, both macroeconomic and microeconomic, and the advent of financial inclusion and microbusiness in the Internet age has played its role.

We are now entering the Sustainable Development Goal (SDG) era, in which SDG 1 will be to end extreme poverty in the coming generation. Once again, both macro and micro interventions will be needed for success. Large-scale investments in infrastructure, health systems, and education systems will need to be combined with millions upon millions of start-up companies across Africa, Asia, and the Americas.

The information revolution will give local entrepreneurs new tools and empowerment to get the job done. When they build their businesses, tap into capital markets, and create new applications to address local needs, they will be following in the path that Muhammad Yunus and Jessica Jackley have helped to chart. And when millions of today's young people take up the thrilling task of being the generation that finally ends the ancient scourge of extreme poverty, they will do well to draw from the heart, soul, and mind of Jessica Jackley. This wonderful book will be a companion for countless new young leaders in the fight against poverty in the years ahead.

Patrick the Brickmaker

SOMETHING FROM NOTHING

Eastern Uganda
2004

Patrick didn't have much. As a boy, he lost most of his family when a militant rebel group attacked his village in northern Uganda. He and his younger brother fled the only home they had ever known and headed south. Patrick was unsure where they would end up, but after weeks of traveling they settled in a village near the Uganda-Kenya border, where they came across some distant cousins. They wanted to be as close as they could to family—any family at all.

Patrick and his brother had no home, no food, no money, not even shoes on their feet. They were young, orphaned, uneducated, homeless, and hungry.

It would have been easy for Patrick to look at his life and count the things he had lost. It would have been easy for him to view himself as a helpless victim, as someone who had been dealt too much injustice, suffered too much loss, and experienced too much pain to fight for a better life for himself. He could have assumed that because he had nothing, he was nothing—and would never become more.

But one morning Patrick made a simple decision that changed everything.

Sitting on the ground, watching the sun rise as he leaned against the side of the mud structure where he slept, he wondered, as he did every morning, whether he would eat that day. He rested his hand on the warm, dry earth. His gaze shifted from the sky to his hand, and he stared at the ground beneath his fingers. An idea began to take shape. In a moment of inspiration, he rolled up his sleeves and he began to dig.

He used a thick, short piece of wood and some scraps of discarded metal as tools. As he dug, he learned. He saw that certain patches of rust-colored earth were harder and contained more clay than others. He experimented, and found that if he mixed the clay with water until it was the right consistency, it could be shaped. Slowly, with his bare hands and a single scrap of wood, he began to work the clay into bricks.

His first attempts produced meager results. The bricks were rough, misshapen, and cracked and crumbled easily. But he kept at it. Soon some of the bricks were good enough to sell, though just for a fraction of a penny each.

He saved some money over the following weeks until he was able to afford a wooden brick mold. The bricks he made with the mold were far better than his first batches; these were smoother and more uniform. They sold for a little more.

Patrick initially let his bricks dry in the sun, but he knew that they could be made stronger if they were fired. So he saved more money and bought a book of matches, gathered some kindling, and stacked his bricks around it to create a self-contained kiln. The kiln-baked bricks sold for even more.

Eventually he could afford a shovel and a trowel to replace his homemade implements. After that, he bought charcoal instead of wood for his fire. Soon he had enough work and enough money to hire his brother. After that, he hired a neighbor. Then another. By the time I met Patrick, in the spring of 2004, he employed several people, had a thriving business, and had built a lovely new home for himself—out of his very own baked mud bricks.

The moment that Patrick began to dig was the moment he began to create a new life for himself. Patrick saw opportunity where others saw none—in the ground beneath his feet—and he saw potential within himself, despite all he lacked. Pulling from the earth one brick at a time, Patrick became an entrepreneur and built his future.

The Pursuit

In 2005, I co-founded Kiva, the world's first personal microlending platform. Through Kiva, individuals can lend small amounts of money—as little as $25 at a time—to other people around the world in need of the funding to start or grow a microenterprise. Since its founding, Kiva, an organization that champions entrepreneurship worldwide, has facilitated over $600 million in loans, helping to lift millions of people out of poverty. Those loans have connected lenders and borrowers in nearly every country on the planet.

Since Kiva, I have gone on to found other companies, including Pro-Founder, a platform that helped entrepreneurs raise investment capital for their start-ups or small businesses from their friends, family, and communities. I've also served as an investor and venture partner at the Collaborative Fund, a seed-stage venture fund focused on investing in creative entrepreneurs who support the sharing economy and the idea of collaborative consumption. The companies we support are helping to build a movement away from ownership-based economy and toward an access- or sharing-based economy. Additionally, I speak about entrepreneurship to thousands of people each year, at universities, businesses, conferences, and myriad other groups all over the world. For the last fifteen years, entrepreneurship has been at the heart of everything I do.

The funny thing is, for most of my life, I had no interest in entrepreneurship—or more accurately, I had no interest in what I assumed entrepreneurship was all about. I didn't care much about the kinds of things I thought entrepreneurs should obsess over. For instance, I didn't feel a burning need to start my own venture; I believed I could do a great deal of good by serving in a leadership role in an existing organization or the public sector. I didn't care much about making a ton of money; instead I cared about helping people, which often seemed to involve giving money away. My professional idols were not CEOs who had started and scaled for-profit companies; I was much more interested in Peace Corps volunteers who spent their days in far-flung places, perhaps working with just one small village at a time.

Plus, the entrepreneurs who seemed to rule the start-up world were mostly men, they were focused on high tech, and they chose to solve problems for privileged people that I thought could hardly be categorized as real "problems" in the first place. I didn't relate to those entrepreneurs and had no interest in working on their ventures. And in any case, there was something about the entrepreneurial path that just seemed out of my reach. I had no idea how to go about sourcing venture capital funding, accessing some cutting-edge information and research that might help me create the next big thing, getting some famous mentor to take me under his wing, gaining official institutional support, or any of those kinds of mysterious feats that seemed to be crucial parts of the process for successful entrepreneurs.

Then, after college, I moved to Silicon Valley, one of the most entrepreneurial places on the planet, and began working at the Stanford Graduate School of Business (Stanford GSB). Suddenly, I was constantly surrounded by ideas about entrepreneurship. Through this immersion, many of my old stereotypes quickly fell away. My assumptions as to what entrepreneurship was about—solely making money, starting a business simply to start a business, solving trivial "problems," and the like—

began to be replaced by other, more hopeful interpretations of what entrepreneurship could be.

For instance, I learned that there were start-up ventures of all kinds: for profit, for purpose, and everything in between. I learned that there were founders of all kinds too, each with unique motivations for building their organizations. Most conversations at the Stanford GSB were as much about social change and social impact as about financial success.

I began to wake up to the potential of entrepreneurship to be a powerful force for positive change in the world. And for the first time, I was intrigued. I was drawn to it. I actually thought that maybe entrepreneurship could have something to do with my life.

Perhaps more importantly, I found a community of people who genuinely cared about solving the same problems I wanted to solve, and seemed to be doing so in a thoughtful, strategic, and highly effective way as social entrepreneurs. Students, professors, colleagues, and others I got to know at Stanford challenged and encouraged me to pursue the things I cared about most in an entrepreneurial way. They inspired me to make my own path.

In the spring of 2004, that path led me to East Africa to work with people living in poverty who, through their own entrepreneurial paths, were overcoming their circumstances and building a better life for themselves. I spent three and a half months in Kenya, Uganda, and Tanzania, interviewing entrepreneurs unlike any I had encountered in Silicon Valley. I met farmers, fishermen, charcoal sellers, rickshaw drivers, basket weavers, shopkeepers, shepherds, seamstresses, and many other hardworking people who, despite living in abject poverty, were building microenterprises to create a more sustainable source of income for their families. They were people like Patrick, the brickmaker, and they quickly became heroes to me.

These entrepreneurs built their enterprises in the most unlikely, most unexpected, harshest environments imaginable. Yet despite their meager circumstances, they created and pursued opportunities to improve life for themselves and their families. Many built businesses big enough to support their own households, and some went beyond this, creating jobs for others in their communities or inspiring others to strive for more, catalyzing growth among dozens of others in their village. These entrepreneurs did so much with so little, succeeding with no access to the kinds of resources or advantages I had always assumed entrepreneurs required to move forward.

While I arrived in East Africa with a spark of interest in entrepreneurship, the people I met there fanned that spark into an intense blaze. They inspired the creation of Kiva. And they have served as a source of motivation for me every day since. In fact, what I learned—and continue to learn—from the Patricks of the world influences my thinking on the topic of entrepreneurship in a way nothing else has.

They embody my favorite definition of entrepreneurship, which comes from Harvard Business School professor Howard Stevenson: "Entrepreneurship is the pursuit of opportunity without regard to resources currently controlled." In other words, entrepreneurship is the ability to pursue opportunity without money, or permission, or pedigree, or most other means that might make the pursuit easier. Stevenson emphasizes the *pursuit* without regard to *possessions*. As I see it, his definition hints at this truth: The heart of entrepreneurship is never about what we have. It's about what we do.

I thought I understood this before hearing firsthand stories like Patrick's. But I didn't. Perhaps it was seeing firsthand the extremely tough circumstances in which those entrepreneurs thrived—circumstances that included abjectly few resources, vastly less than even the scrappiest start-up in a Silicon Valley garage would have—that finally made me understand the power of this concept. I had encountered living proof that even someone living in a mud hut could launch a venture. I now knew that even a person who had not been formally educated past grade school could start a microenterprise and make a modest living from it. I had come face-to-face with real people who, despite their lack of experience, expertise, power, money, popularity, or approval, had succeeded on their own terms as entrepreneurs. I had met Patrick, who had only the dirt beneath his bare feet and yet chose to act, building his business brick by brick.

I became convinced that great entrepreneurs have this in common: They simply make a series of choices, day after day, to move forward regardless of what they lack or must fight against.

It was thanks to this realization that I began to envision a new path for myself as well. I came to truly believe that if I worked hard enough and chose to keep pushing myself forward despite my own weakness, disadvantages, and obstacles, maybe I could become an entrepreneur too.

To be clear, I would never suggest that overcoming poverty is simply a matter of a change in perspective or attitude. I do believe, though, that any person can choose to think in a more hopeful, optimistic, entrepreneurial way, and that this kind of mind-set paired with consistent entrepreneurial action is vital to building a better life—whether from a starting point of desperation or of privilege. I believe that a path of entrepreneurship is a path that is accessible to anyone, anywhere.

I wrote this book not solely for those who call themselves entrepreneurs per se, and not just for those who want to start an organization of their own from scratch. This book is for anyone who wants to be inspired to make progress toward their dreams despite the challenges standing in their way. It is for anyone who wants to spend each day tapped into the kind of energy, creativity, and passion that the best entrepreneurs in the world embody. It is for anyone who wants to live and work in a more opportunity-finding, solution-building way.

Over the last fifteen years, I have had the pleasure of meeting hundreds of entrepreneurs around the world. In the pages that follow, I share stories from my own entrepreneurial journey alongside the stories of a chicken farmer, a shopkeeper, a hairdresser, a goatherd, and many other inspiring entrepreneurs I've encountered along the way. They are stories that I have revisited again and again in my life because they remind me to believe in the possibility of overcoming any obstacle, whether external or internal, standing in the way of what I want to achieve. They remind me not to be held back by what I lack, what I have lost, or where

I have failed. They remind me to pursue my own dreams even when it feels like I don't have enough of one thing or another . . . or that I don't know enough . . . or, in so many words, that *I* am not enough. They remind me that the greatest entrepreneurs succeed not because of what they possess but because of what they are determined to do.

To be clear, some of these stories are great business successes, in which real people have had genuine "rags to riches" journeys. And some stories are special because those entrepreneurs taught me a crucial lesson that I needed to learn along my own journey, such as how to see opportunity in an unexpected place, how to empower other people, or how to believe in myself. My goal in sharing their stories, and my own, is a simple one: to inspire you to live a more entrepreneurial life. I believe we can all achieve a more hopeful, more creative, and more positive existence together by realizing the incredible entrepreneurial potential that exists in every human being on this planet—especially the one reading this book.

Clay
Water
Brick

CHAPTER 1

Find the Courage to Question

The Poor with Us

Our Sunday school teacher read, as she did every week, from the Good News Bible. She told us about Jesus: about what he said and did, about the big and small miracles, about how to live a good life. I listened intently as I sat cross-legged on my carpet square, one of a dozen fuzzy islands floating on a sea of linoleum tiles. Behind her, a construction paper chart was taped to the wall, with the names of all the students in class, each with some number of gold stars next to the name. I stared at the stars lined up next to my name, one for every time I had done well (I'd earned my newest one for memorizing the Twenty-third Psalm), counting them over and over again, and comparing my ranking among the other kids. I imagined the stars were my team of cheerleaders, each standing on two pointy legs with a pointy head and two pointy arms outstretched right and left. I was five and a half years old and wanted nothing more than to be good. A good daughter, a good sister, a good student, a good everything.

On this particular Sunday, my teacher was talking about poverty. She explained that people living in poverty did not have even the most basic things they needed, like food or clothing or shelter. She told us that Jesus loved the poor and wanted everyone else to love them too. Reading from the Bible in a scattershot way, she jumped around from story to story. One was about a widow giving the last of her coins at church; another was about someone called a Samaritan who helped a sick man on the side of the road; another was about someone pouring perfume on Jesus' feet. Some of the stories made sense to me. Many did not.

I tried to follow along in my own Bible, a hardcover G-rated children's version with an oversized font and colorful illustrations. It was the biggest book I owned, and therefore felt like the most important. I flipped through it carefully, looking at the cartoon drawings, keeping an eye out for pictures of the kinds of people my Sunday school teacher was talking about: the poor. In some scenes they were pale and gaunt, down on their knees, their arms reaching up to a bright, sunny heaven for help. In others they were barefoot and filthy, with rags for clothing. They were people shouting in pain, wounded black and blue, or sick with white, leprous skin; people crying, bandages spotted with red across their eyes, chest, head, or hands; people on stretchers, green with nausea or gray with death.

As I stared at the pictures, my Sunday school teacher quoted Jesus, saying, "What you do for the least of these you do for me."

Her words made me stop and look up.

For a child who wanted nothing more than to do well by her parents and teachers, the idea that I could be some sort of cosmic helper was the most motivating thing I had ever heard! *Helping the poor was helping God Himself.* I felt I had just been given the world's greatest homework assignment. I would get this right. I wanted more stars. Big ones.

My mind raced with questions about how this was supposed to work. Where were these poor people? How exactly should I help? How did God keep track of how well I was doing? Did the poor report back up to heaven when I gave them my things—sort of like how (according to my mom) the myriad Santas at the mall reported back to the one real Santa at the North Pole what I wanted for Christmas? Would I be docked points if I handed over only the stuff I didn't want, like the crayons in

colors I never used, or the half of my sandwich that had less peanut but-
ter and jelly on it, and kept all my favorite things for myself? Or was
every poor person actually God himself, like Jesus had been, since God
could be everywhere and was, apparently, good at disguises?

As the litany ran through my head, my Sunday school teacher told us
something else that Jesus said, something that again stopped me cold.
She said, as if it was no big deal at all, that Jesus promised, "The poor will
always be with us."

My stomach knotted. I felt confused, then angry, then scared as this
sunk in. Why would God make poor people stay poor forever? Couldn't
God make the world however he wanted? And what did this mean for
me? Were my plans to help the poor destined to be inadequate? Was
Jesus setting me up to fail?

A terrifying scenario began to form in my head. I saw a long line of
poor people in front of me, one after another after another, each in need
of something I had. One was asking for my coat; one wanted my softest
blanket. Another insisted I hand over the azure-blue crayon I loved. Two
others wanted not just half my PB and J sandwich, but all of it. Every
time I gave something to one of these people, they would say "thank
you," but then they would make the long walk back to the end of the line,
using up my crayon and gobbling my sandwich on the way, and then
they would take their place again so they could return to me for more.
Because, after all, the poor would always be with us. With me. They
would never stop needing and they would never go away. They would
follow me around everywhere I went, asking for something else, something more. Their poverty would be endless. No matter how much I
gave, it would never be enough.

Jesus said so.

The Cost of a Cup of Coffee

As I got older, I heard other stories that convinced me the problem of
poverty was enormous. These stories reiterated the notion that poverty

could never really be solved, not completely. They assured me that, while it was nice to try, no one could ever really help enough or fix things well enough to make a permanent difference.

Over time the illustrations of the poor in my Good News Bible were replaced with the much more real and far more intense images I saw in mailings from charity organizations, or in the newspapers and magazines that came to our house: people pleading for help, their arms outstretched to the camera, alongside headlines of disaster or disease; men with fists raised in riot, alongside news of oppression or war; women fleeing from fighting and famine; children with swollen bellies lying in makeshift hospital rooms; babies like skeletons, their rib cages and collarbones just beneath a thin layer of skin, with flies perched on the edges of their sunken eyelids. Everyone, and everything around them, seemed dirty, broken, angry, empty.

These images convinced me that the poor lived very far away from me. My neighborhood in the suburbs of Pittsburgh, Pennsylvania, seemed like a fairy tale in comparison. None of the kids I knew looked like those I saw in these photographs. Everyone around me looked healthy and well fed. I lived in a modern Norman Rockwell painting of soft front lawns and big shady trees with perennial flowers circling their trunks. The front doors of the houses on my street were swung open in the summer and decorated with holly and wreaths in the wintertime. Hopscotch chalk lines stained the sidewalks. Bicycles and scooters lay strewn across front yards. Minivans were parked neatly in driveways.

I could not imagine the poor existing in the only world I knew. How could anyone go hungry when every kitchen I had ever seen had a full fridge and a crowded pantry? How could anyone be homeless when even my neighbors' dogs had doghouses, and where even the mail had nice mailboxes to sit in? How could it be that not everyone had a warm jacket when everyone in my family had both winter clothes and summer clothes, and even different shoes for school and soccer practice and church?

So when stories about poor people infiltrated my idyllic existence, they caught my attention. I tried hard to imagine those people and to process the statistics that accompanied the stories. Half of the world was living on less than $2 a day. Twenty-two thousand children were dying each day *from poverty*. Nearly a billion people were unable to read a book or sign their names. These enormous, haunting numbers were impossible for my brain to fathom, so my heart took over. I felt anger, sadness, fear, guilt, even shame about my own relative wealth and privilege as a white, middle-class American kid.

Of course, this was exactly the desired effect of the well-intentioned nonprofits vying for my attention in their marketing campaigns. They counted on their messages to make me feel something, and then they relied on my ability to translate those feelings into action: The worse I felt, the more I should want to give. Then, just when I thought I couldn't take any more sad statistics, the nonprofit offered a way out: Donate! Give! Help!

Who could say no? All I had to do was pick up the phone, dial the 1-800 number on the screen, and I would be connected with someone who could solve these problems (via check, credit card, or money order)! If I just emptied my pockets or dug through my couch cushions for loose change, I'd find enough to extend a child's life for one more day! If I could spare even the smallest amount—Sally Struthers and other passionate spokespeople told me that "less than the cost of a cup of coffee" was enough—I could be a part of their game-changing work! For just a few dollars I could become the solution!

And so I gave. I dug for lost coins. I took my weekly allowance to church and stuffed it into the velvety bag that was passed around to collect the congregation's tithes. And I got others to give too. I hawked Dixie cups half-full of watery Kool-Aid from a card table on my front lawn. I sold magazine subscriptions and cookies and gigantic chocolate bars door-to-door. I toted my UNICEF box around the neighborhood on Halloween night. And every once in a while, my mom would take me to the local bank, which would tally the change, and then my mom would send a check and my handwritten notes to the poor kids I had seen on TV.

Each time I did these things, I felt a little bit better. At least for a while.

Part of me knew that giving a few dollars here and there was a cheap replacement for what I really sought. Deep down, I knew that I would never be satisfied until I could make some sort of real contact with the people I felt obligated to serve. In fact, I was becoming more and more certain that the strange cycle of giving in which I'd been participating actually made me feel more disconnected from the actual human beings I felt called to help. Instead of experiencing a real, meaningful interaction with a needy person, I was participating in a series of economic transactions with large organizations that had convinced me they knew how to fix things. I wasn't actually allowed to hand over my PB and J sandwich. I was just funding someone else's grocery list. It was all incredibly unsatisfying.

The follow-up letters from those nonprofits thanking me for my donations added insult to injury. I got form letters in the mail (usually addressed to my mom, who had written the check) thanking her for the donation in the first sentence and then immediately asking for more. As a caricature of personal touch, there were often ink-jet printed signatures of people I had never heard of and had not intended to give any money to. (What was an executive director? Why wasn't the letter signed by Jamal in Ethiopia or Vilma in Guatemala, the kids from the infomercials?) Some organizations even went so far as to make the form letters look like they had little notes scrawled in the margins, as if their donors would be fooled by a "handwriting" font. Even as a kid I knew what was happening. I was being thanked by a computer.

I saved one of the most confusing, dissonant thank-you letters I received back then. For a while it hung taped to the wall above my desk. The letter came in response to a donation I had sent to a nonprofit organization specializing in medical procedures for babies born with cleft lips and palates. Along with a standard one-page thank-you note expressing how valuable my support was to the organization, I received a self-addressed envelope for an additional donation. So far, nothing new. But the envelope stood out. On it was a photograph, the face of a baby who had been born with a cleft lip, which had left a gaping hole from her mouth to her right nostril. Bafflingly, next to the picture—after I had just been told how much the organization appreciated every penny, and how much of a difference each contribution made—was a special offer: "Make one gift now, and we'll never ask for another donation again."

The campaign was as offensive to me as it was resonant, revealing an intimate understanding of the love/hate relationship that can unfold between well-intentioned donors and well-intentioned nonprofits. On the one hand, I knew every dollar was appreciated and would make a big difference. That part felt great. On the other hand, someone in that organization guessed that after a while, making an impact through their particular program would probably lose its thrill. Another few bucks, another smile repaired. Seen one, seen them all, right? So they decided to cut to the chase. Their message told me: "Hey donor, we get it. We're bothering you. So let's quit while we're ahead. Pay us off and you can go on with your life."

In a world with infinite need, with no such thing as "enough," this organization seemed to understand that no donor could give forever.

Sadly, I couldn't disagree. I had become convinced that it was impossible to give enough, to cause enough change, to care enough. So I still gave, but I did so knowing exactly what I was doing. I wasn't just buying the privilege to change someone else's life with my donation. I was buying a temporary sense of relief for myself. With each transaction, even that feeling of temporary reprieve became more and more fleeting. I knew I wouldn't be able to keep up with all of the world's requests for my spare change. It was just like the long line of poor people I had pictured in Sunday school, following me around forever.

Naturally, slowly, I began to shut down inside. My heart began to harden a little. What else could I do but distance myself? I paid less and less attention to the infomercials. I stopped trying so hard to comprehend the big scary statistics. I changed the channel before I could see the 1-800 number flash across the screen (even though at that point I had it memorized). I learned how to tune out, so that the information wouldn't sink in so deeply—and so I wouldn't be constantly disappointed by my failure to help.

Whitewashed

By the time I reached high school, my relationship with giving was like a bad breakup that wouldn't stick: perpetually on-again, off-again, with plenty of dramatic highs and lows in between. Despite my frequent frustration, I was still in love with the idea of saving the world, so I kept coming back to give it yet another try.

However, by now I had become significantly less interested in just donating money. I wanted to participate. I wanted to help actually distribute whatever it was my donations had been buying. I wanted to get to hand over that damn PB and J myself. Even if the solutions themselves were temporary, or even flawed, I craved knowing what it felt like to deliver them personally, with my own two hands. So I gave of my time instead of my money. I started volunteering, though not in a very strategic way. I asked around and jumped at whatever came along. Unfortunately, most of these experiences left me feeling just as confused and unsatisfied as before.

For instance, I signed up to volunteer after school at the local hospital as a candy striper, but instead of interacting with patients, I ended up manning the gift shop or coffee stand. Was I just free labor? Another time, I volunteered for Special Olympics, helping to coach kids on the swim team. While we all had a blast, it was such a popular volunteer opportunity that there were many more coaches than Olympians. Did my presence matter to anyone but me? Later, I served dinners to hungry families at a local soup kitchen. At first I was satisfied by the close contact and obvious impact I had. But after just a few visits, the people walking through the line holding their plates became familiar. I remember one gentleman asking me, as I wiped down a table, "See you tomorrow?" His question was harmless but I began to feel critical. Did he *want* to come back for his meals day after day, week after week, year after year? Did I want to serve him indefinitely? Was scooping instant mashed potatoes onto plates the best use of everyone's time? What about breaking the cycle of hunger? How could we do that instead?

A particularly bewildering volunteer experience happened when I signed up to spend part of my weekend fixing up the homes of economically disadvantaged people living in inner-city Pittsburgh. I worked with a local nonprofit community organization that spearheaded several economic development initiatives in the city, including deploying volunteers to do free home repairs for in-need homeowners.

Early one hot, humid Saturday morning, half a dozen high school friends and I climbed into a van in our church parking lot and schlepped ourselves and a bunch of supplies downtown. At the organization's headquarters, we were given an address along with a list of projects that needed to be done there. We drove to the address we had been given and knocked, and although there was no answer at the front door, we unloaded paint cans and brushes and drop cloths and began to work.

Together, our team of mostly small-framed teenage girls managed to awkwardly lift a long metal ladder around to the back of the house so that, per our instructions, we could whitewash the back porch. My head was down as I walked. I was breathing heavily and sweating. My arms were shaking from the heavy lifting. I was so focused on not dropping my section of the ladder that I didn't look up until we were a few feet from the porch. That's when I heard a muffled bass beat. Sitting on a lawn chair in the grass next to the porch was a handsome, muscled twentysomething man in a white undershirt and mesh shorts. His feet rested on a stump, and his chair leaned back at an angle so that only its back legs touched the ground. He had a nice collection of 1980s technology: puffy foam headphones connected to a Walkman, and a Gameboy in his hands. There was a glass of soda pop next to him too, with lots of ice, dripping on the outside from the heat. I was staring at the glass when he spoke.

"Hey, uh, everyone. Thanks for coming. It's that wall over there." And with that he gestured to the wall by the porch, which had been partially covered with graffiti. For the next four hours our church group whitewashed the side of the house, sweating in the heat, while the young man sat in his lawn chair playing video games. Now and then he got up to walk alongside the house and talk on a cordless phone. But mostly he just sat there, looking up from his game every once in a while, smiling at us. Once he gave us a thumbs-up. Another time, I thought, he chuckled to himself. My cheeks burned red, from the sun and heat, but also from confusion and embarrassment.

The young man seemed perfectly nice. And the truth is, we didn't know who he was (and for some reason no one bothered to find out). It's possible that he lived in the home we were working on. Perhaps he was the son or grandson of the homeowners. Maybe he was just a neighbor who had agreed to supervise our work while the owner was out. Of course, at the time, I could only feel frustrated. Why wasn't he painting too? He certainly looked like he could lift the paint cans and whitewash a wall much faster than I could. I left that day wondering: Who decides who really needs help anyway?

Dozens of other volunteering attempts and a few years later, I still felt stuck. Even experiences that felt rewarding in the moment often left me feeling empty in the long run. I questioned what kind of permanent change I had made, or if that kind of impact was even possible. Instead of getting closer to finding answers, I seemed to keep adding to my growing list of questions.

But then, I came across an opportunity unlike anything I had experienced before. I hoped it was different enough to help me finally find some answers.

Port-au-Prince to Prom

When I was a senior in high school, I overheard some friends talking about a spring break service trip to Haiti to work in an orphanage. I couldn't believe it. Haiti. The poorest country in the southern hemisphere. Surely I could do something useful in an environment with so much need.

When I mentioned the idea of going to Haiti to my parents over dinner that night, they didn't drop their forks and knives in shock the way some of my other friends' parents did. They listened and asked questions. And they kept asking questions. And then sure enough, a few weeks later, I was packing my bags for Haiti. So was my dad. (The one condition of my parents' approval was that he come along too.)

For the kids at the orphanage, I packed toys, soap, socks, and toothbrushes. For myself, I packed mosquito repellent, hiking boots, some T-shirts, and a few skirts long enough to cover my ankles. The orphanage was run by two women who had gone to Bob Jones University and had brought the school's extremely conservative culture with them from Greenville, South Carolina. That meant shorts and shoulder-baring tank tops were not allowed, despite the sweltering heat.

I remember the week that followed in bits and pieces.

My stomach flip-flopped during the flight from Miami to Cap Haitien, a deafening and jolting ride on a cargo plane. That morning, just for our flight, exactly one seat for each passenger had been temporarily bolted to the floor. There was no bathroom, which we learned only after someone had an emergency mid-flight. When we touched down and the plane door opened, it felt like being smacked with a wave of damp heat, burning my lungs when I breathed. During the subsequent ride from the airport to the orphanage, all fourteen of us piled into the back of a pickup truck, zipping through the chaos of Cap Haitien traffic and then bouncing along unpaved roads, past barren-looking fields, to a plain rectangular building made of concrete blocks with an iron sheet roof, surrounded by a ten-foot-high concrete wall with shards of broken glass on top.

I remember meeting the kids for the first time, bearing our care packages proudly in opened cardboard boxes that customs agents had rifled through. We said hello to one another briefly but soon their attention became sharply focused on the boxes, not us, so in turn our attention became focused on watching the kids open each item. While their reactions were completely appropriate—delighted at a toy, disappointed at socks in the wrong size, bored by the soap and toothbrush—I found myself judging them. I thought they ought to be grateful for all of our offerings. And then I judged myself, sneaking away later to cry and pray, asking God to forgive me.

I remember how proud I felt serving as the designated translator with everyone we met, since I was the only one in our group who spoke French (which was close enough to Haitian Creole to get by). I felt even more pride because, for the first time, aside from when I'd gone camping with my family as a kid, I was roughing it, living without running water or electricity. We showered during afternoon rainstorms, fully clothed, under a break in the building's gutter, jumping into and out of the makeshift waterfall when the thunder and lightning let up. We used candles and flashlights at night.

I remember the soft, musical sounds of a roomful of children doing arts and crafts with the supplies we had brought. They were clearly happy, and yet I couldn't shake the panicky, unsettled feeling that for every Popsicle stick and pipe cleaner we had brought along, we could have instead brought an extra toothbrush for people outside the orphanage. Or vitamins. Or books.

On the day before we left, we all cried as though we had known each other forever. We exchanged addresses and promised to write. Some kids from the orphanage gave away their only photographs of themselves so we would not forget their faces. I had been given two such photos, and vowed to put them in a place where I would see them every day. I carefully tucked them into my Bible to protect them on the journey home.

We flew back to Miami early on Easter morning. My dad and I attended a sunrise service on the beach before catching the next flight home to Pittsburgh. Naturally, the sermon focused on how Jesus had taken our place and died for our sins, and had then been resurrected. I thought about how so many of my new friends in Haiti would have gladly taken my place that morning, flying across the ocean to the United States, and sobbed knowing how unwilling I would have been to take theirs. Later that same day, I was at home in my bedroom, unpacking. I unzipped my backpack, horrified to find the well-worn Good Book, with its translucent pages and soft spine, sitting slumped at the bottom. The photos lay beneath it, badly bent, stuck together, and slimy from a tube of lip gloss that had melted in the heat.

The following weekend was my high school's senior prom. I was obsessed with my poufy dress, wanted to ride in a limo with my friends, and loved all the fuss around this extravagant rite of passage. Yet I also felt like a complete hypocrite. How could I be part of something so frivolous and wasteful? What could the money spent on my dress have bought for my friends in Haiti instead? What would they think of me if they knew what I was doing?

Prom came and went. Days, then weeks, went by. Despite my efforts not to, I reassimilated to my old life. I stopped crying so much. I stopped having panic attacks when I walked into a mini-mall or fully stocked grocery store, aware that many of the people I had met in Haiti probably wouldn't even believe places like these existed. I marveled less and less at the things in my house that had seemed amazing upon my initial return, like the TV, microwave, and hot running water. I bought new things that I didn't really need and forgot to feel bad about it. I stopped writing my Haitian pen pals.

A few months later, I left for college at Bucknell University, situated just a few hours' drive from my family, in beautiful Amish country. At that point, heartbroken and a little numb post-Haiti, I doubted if the problem of poverty could ever be solved. I still wanted to make a valiant effort, though, and my emotional detachment forced my head to take over where my heart left off. So over the next four years, I studied philosophy, political science, and poetry in an attempt to learn how to ask the right questions, understand power, and harness language, respectively—all as part of an attempt to understand poverty and to equip myself to fight against it. By the time I graduated I had a lot to say about development tactics and techniques. I had strong opinions on what did and didn't work. I could talk to people who cared about the same issues I cared about in an educated way. My informed skepticism made me sound smart and levelheaded about social problems. And I was. I just wasn't tapping into the same passion that I'd once had.

To be fair, my undergraduate years were not devoid of emotion, and there were a handful of notable high points that ended up making a lasting impact. I continued my volunteer efforts locally, deepening my understanding of rural poverty. During the summer before my sophomore year, I interned at World Vision and gained a new appreciation for how hard it is to be on the other side of the nonprofit fund-raising process. Most significantly, during the spring of my junior year, I had an eye-opening study abroad experience through Semester at Sea—the one-hundred-day voyage included stops in ten countries as we circled the planet. While that voyage continues to serve as a reference point and touchstone in my understanding of the world, the short-term effect it had on me was much like my trip to Haiti years before: I emerged from each new country deeply moved but just as uncertain about how to stay connected to those brief, powerful encounters.

So when I graduated, I felt book-smart but still nowhere near street-smart about poverty. I still did not know what I should be doing to help the poor. This lack of clarity around graduation time made finding a job somewhat challenging; I wasn't sure what I was searching for, so I couldn't look very hard. But I did know one thing. I had fallen in love with a boy who lived in California, and this was a force much more powerful than any employment prospects on the East Coast. So, giddy and optimistic, I decided to just go west and have an adventure instead.

Katherine the Fishmonger

GO TO THE LAKE

Tororo, Uganda
2005

Katherine jumped and sang, clapping her hands and ululating
to welcome me back to Tororo. Awkwardly, a cameraman from
PBS's *Frontline/World* hovered a few feet away, filming the entire thing for an upcoming fifteen-minute documentary on
Kiva. Katherine didn't seem to mind one bit. She ran toward
me and hugged me, beaming. I had not seen her for a year,
and she knew I had returned to check in on her and the
progress she had made since she had received—and repaid—
a $500 loan. She held my hands and we walked over to a
clearing near her house, where we sat in the shade so she
could fill me in on the events of the past year. She had so
much good news to share.

I had first met Katherine Opio in the spring of 2004 and
was immediately struck by her charisma. The woman knew
how to sell. She was persuasive, confident, and insistent. For
years, she had sold onions, tomatoes, greens, and cooking oil
to her neighbors in her village outside of Tororo, Uganda. But
although she worked hard and had a natural talent for sales,

she and her seven children barely survived on her meager profits. As a widow, she alone was responsible for keeping her family alive.

Things began to change for Katherine when, in 2000, she received a $100 grant and business training from Village Enterprise, a California-based nonprofit focused on sustainable microenterprise development in villages throughout East Africa. The course taught her about choosing the best business opportunities, marketing, bookkeeping, and other strategies to succeed. What she learned inspired her to switch from selling vegetables and cooking oil to selling fish. She knew there was a great demand for fish in her village, and she saw an opportunity to sell at a lower price than others around her.

At first Katherine purchased about a half-dozen fish at a time from a middleman and sold them from a roadside stand. But day after day she felt frustrated, knowing she was paying the middleman much more than she would if she could buy from a fisherman directly.

But to do this, she would have to go to the lake.

For a villager living near Tororo, Uganda, a trip to Lake Victoria was not without cost or risk. Few people in her village had ever made the journey. Most residents in Katherine's poverty-plagued community were born, lived, and died in the same place, with very few experiences taking place beyond a single day's walking distance. The journey to the lake was about 100 kilometers, well over an hour by car. Bus or taxi fare could be equivalent to a day's wages. And activity in the marketplaces and trading centers near Tororo started early, so for Katherine a few hours driving back and forth from the lake could mean losing precious morning hours selling her wares. Plus, there was no guarantee that the fish Katherine purchased at the lake would be priced low enough to justify all the time and effort spent.

And yet Katherine decided to take the risk and go.

She was nervous the entire morning's ride to Lake Victoria. She had no idea what awaited her, and wondered if the trip would be worth it. Hours later, Katherine was hauling a whole basketful of fish back to her village. She then sold them all, in her own village and in other villages around Tororo. Her profits nearly tripled.

Katherine went back to the lake frequently over the following weeks, and continued to adjust her business model. During the next rainy season, she saw a new opportunity emerge: fish were suddenly abundant and prices dropped, so she bought fish in bulk and smoked some of them, allowing her not only to charge more but to reach different customers than she usually did, including middlemen who used to sell to her.

Katherine's progress was due to her hard work, and catalyzed by the loans she had received, but I believe that most of all, Katherine had moved ahead in her life because she had been willing to take a risk. She had gone to the lake to see for herself what was there.

CHAPTER 2

Bravely Go

The First Valley

I landed in San Francisco with two suitcases and zero plan. All I knew was that I was going to live with a group of friends in a house on Sand Hill Road in Palo Alto. To anyone who has spent time in Silicon Valley, the name of this road is significant. If an entrepreneur says she is going "up and down Sand Hill Road" it means one thing: She is fund-raising for her start-up company, as the majority of the Valley's venture capital offices are concentrated on Sand Hill. Of course, I didn't know this at the time. I was just happy to have a place to crash. (Later on, my roommates and I would seriously consider starting a VC firm simply because we had such a valuable address.)

That house, number 2010, was home to a dozen recent graduates crammed into every possible space. My friend Sundeep, a successful entrepreneur today, lived in a closet-sized space next to our kitchen. Jon, who went on to work at Kiva for many years, lived in the garage with his cat, Zeke, who was of course not allowed according to the lease. Graham lived in the corner of the living room behind a sheet that was nailed to the ceiling, and yet another friend pitched a tent in the backyard and paid $50 each month to use the bathroom. I lived with several other girls in the biggest room; our beds barely fit, but we managed to line them up against the walls, mattresses head to head, toe to toe, and so on like dominoes. Most important to me at the time, the house was walking distance from where Matt Flannery lived. Matt and I had met during our senior years of college—mine at Bucknell, his at Stanford—in the spring of 2000. Our paths had crossed at a conference in Washington, D.C. After just a few days of getting to know each other we decided to stay in touch and soon found ourselves in a long-distance relationship. Eventually, I moved to California to shorten that distance.

The day after I landed in California I crammed a pile of copies of my résumé into my backpack and walked across the street, following the line of palm trees that led to Stanford University. As I wandered around campus, I handed a résumé to anyone who would take one, and soon I found myself talking to Julie Juergens at the Stanford Graduate School of Business. Julie, who led the Public Management Program at the Center for Social Innovation, hired me as a temporary administrative assistant for another staff person on medical leave. I was grateful to have a job, any job, since I still didn't know exactly what I wanted to do (and needed to pay my rent while I figured it out).

Actually, that's not completely true. I had an idea of what I wanted to do fifteen or twenty years in the future, but I didn't really know what steps to take to get there. There was no row of palm trees to follow, leading the way toward my big career goals. How did one become an executive director of a great nonprofit? Or a development director, or any of the other big titles I thought I wanted? I had no idea. I just knew I wanted to serve in a leadership role in an organization that had figured out how to effectively and efficiently serve the poor.

Even as I accepted the job with Julie, I felt a little disappointed that I had landed at a business school, of all places. At that time, I still thought that people interested in business were by definition uninterested in solving important social problems. Despite the lofty title of the research department where I was about to begin working—the Center for Social Innovation—I was skeptical about whether business students would use their skills to actually help people. It seemed backward to me. The only thing these people could do, I thought, was make a lot of money and give it away someday, if they ever got to that point. And in my own experience, that cycle had felt unsatisfying and seemed insufficient in the end. I was worried that I was selling out, and that immersing myself in business-school culture would expose me to the wrong values. At best, I thought, the experience would be unpleasant; at worst, it would distract me from getting my big, cosmic questions about poverty answered.

In fact I was so worried about this that I took a second job in the evenings and on weekends at a small nonprofit halfway house in East Palo Alto for teen moms and their children. I served as a live-in "house mom" and on-site manager for the shelter so that I could be sure I'd be among others who truly wanted to help those in need and who saw the world the same way I did.

Bake Sales and Bottom Lines

I lived in the shelter with the residents under my supervision—four teenage girls and their children—in a modest three-bedroom single-story house on a cul-de-sac, backed up against a pocket of the San Francisco Bay near the mouth of the San Francisquito Creek. East Palo Alto contrasts starkly with Palo Alto and Stanford, which are just across the highway: Palo Alto is one of the wealthiest neighborhoods in the entire United States, while East Palo Alto is economically disadvantaged and has significantly more crime than its prosperous neighbors. Things were famously bad during the 1980s and 1990s; in 1992, East Palo Alto had the highest homicide rate in the country. But that was a long time ago. Since then, the city's crime problems have subsided a great deal and the city is changing fast. For better or worse, the region is being gentrified and a full 25 percent of the city has been bought, bulldozed, and built up for newer, wealthier residential areas and retail space. I saw the beginnings of these changes when I volunteered in various capacities at the shelter between 2001 and 2004, and when I lived there for several months in 2003.

While I lived in the house my days were full, to say the least. Every weekday I'd wake up early to help with breakfast and get the girls and kids out the door on time. The girls weren't allowed to be at home unsupervised, so we'd all disperse together each morning and I'd lock the door to the empty house behind us. It was a frenzy of activity to get everyone going. Imagine four looks-conscious teenage girls plus a half-dozen babies and toddlers cycling through a single bathroom, let alone making their way through all the other steps in their morning routines, before leaving the house. Once we were all out the door, a few of the girls would load their little ones into their car seats in my car. Then the girls would make their own way to nearby bus stops and train stations to head to high school or vocational training programs, while I would drop each child off at their respective day-care facilities on my way to Stanford to begin my "real" workday.

While I had had my doubts about what I'd be exposed to at Stanford, in fact there could not have been a better place for me to learn about social change and social impact. I found myself surrounded by people, resources, and ideas that inspired and challenged me. I joined student-led discussions at lunch, and asked students I admired to have coffee with me. I crashed lectures and conferences. I heard famous speakers several evenings a week. Sometimes I read through company case studies that were being used as teaching materials in MBA classes. I even went to the office hours of professors sometimes and, if no one else came to meet with them, I would explain who I was—notably, not an actual, tuition-paying student—and ask if they would be willing to let me ask them questions and learn from them anyway. I don't remember being turned away even once. There was always something to learn or do, and always someone who was willing to talk to me.

At Stanford I learned about organizations that really were changing the world in huge ways. Some organizations were quite large, employing hundreds of people and working in dozens of countries around the world. Some were the most innovative in their industry, whether because they had invented medical technology to save thousands of lives or had pioneered new ways of educating underserved children. All of them seemed smart and well-run, certain of the precise value that every dollar donated or every item sold would produce. Organizations like these and their founders set the bar very high for what it meant to create meaningful, large-scale social change.

On the other hand, the shelter where I lived in East Palo Alto wasn't striving for big, scalable change. Instead, it was intentionally small and focused on the community where it was founded, and it operated like most nonprofits in this country do. Meager funding each year came from just a few sources: foundation grants here and there; donations from wealthy individuals; proceeds from bake sales and garage sales held by board members or other volunteers; and once a year, ticket sales plus whatever was in the offering basket at the end of a Christmas concert at a local church. Overall, the organization made ends meet mostly thanks to the time and money of a few dozen loyal, generous individuals in the community.

At Stanford, the organizations I encountered seemed to measure everything, and could talk intelligently about their impact metrics, Social Return on Investment, and the like. At the shelter, the folks in charge championed the kinds of change that were very hard, if not impossible, to detect. In addition to providing the girls and their babies with a safe place to live, educational activities, career and life coaching, and spiritual mentorship were not just offered but required by the shelter. These programs were run mostly by volunteers who worked in service of an invisible kind of social impact that was supposed to begin with spiritual growth. For instance, staff and board members talked about God "changing the hearts" of the girls and kids through the knowledge and relationships they gained at the shelter, and said that this would lead to a shift in behavior. I thought the idea of changed hearts sounded lovely, but given the other messages I heard at Stanford, I often wondered if the shelter was translating their aspirations into quantifiable goals and permanent impact. For instance, I felt frustrated when I saw girls repeat their choices over and over again, despite the shelter's efforts. One young woman who had lived at the shelter when she was pregnant with her first baby at age fifteen came back pregnant again not just once but twice before she was nineteen years old. She had been through all of the respective programs the organization had to offer and yet she returned again and again. I was baffled. Had there been any meaningful impact at all on this young woman's life beyond providing temporary housing?

Despite all my questions, I loved those girls and their kids, and was deeply moved by the authentic desire and commitment of the organization's leadership to help. So I felt honored when I was asked to participate as a board member and immediately accepted the invitation. However, board meetings often perplexed me and stirred up a mix of competing emotions. We prayed a lot and spoke of beautiful things: of planting seeds in people's hearts, of shepherds and of lost sheep being brought back into the fold, of the weary finding rest and the thirsty drinking the water of life. We spoke of trusting in God's ability to manifest the organization's annual budget, and asked for God's provision in bringing us the people we needed to fill open volunteer and staff positions. We pleaded for God's will to be done, whatever it was, in the lives of the girls whose paths had led them to us. I loved the group's faith and optimism but felt frustrated by a lack of clear answers to some fundamental questions: What exactly were the shelter's goals with each girl who came through the program? What if they failed to meet these goals? How did the organization plan to learn, grow, and become more effective over time? Answers were hard to come by, and it became clear after a while that there was a meaningful disconnect between how I saw the world and how the rest of the group did. Greater enthusiasm existed to repeat annual bake sales, yard sales, and car washes than to try new fundraising methods. The question of why we didn't provide free birth control prompted an awkward silence, then an explanation (from one of the few men on the board) of why the organization didn't support that. I loved the girls and the kids I had gotten to know so deeply, but it became clear that what I thought the organization could become wasn't what the rest of the community would ever want it to be. We weren't a fit for each other—and that was okay. Eventually, I asked a friend to take my place on the board so I could move on.

Just before I was planning to move out of the shelter and into a new apartment, Matt and I went on a weekend hiking trip. In the middle of the mountains, he asked me to marry him. I said yes. As I began to plan our wedding for the following summer, and now with only one job (at Stanford) to focus on, I had time to reflect on what I really wanted next in my life, personally and professionally.

I thought back to my time at the shelter frequently, especially as my perspective continued to be informed by my work at Stanford. Which was better? An organization infused with love and focused on relationships as ends in themselves, even if outcomes were unclear—or large-scale, metrics-driven machines of social change? Where was I better equipped to serve?

My sense was that a combination of these two different approaches would be the best of all worlds. I wondered what it would look like to build an organization based on relationships that could scale far and wide too, that was as smart about its strategy as it was passionate about the people it served. I envisioned an organization that connected individuals to one another in a deeply personal way, and then equipped them to inspire others, serving multitudes more. Could I find—or maybe even help start—something like that?

Micro-Epiphany

The following summer, I took a month off for the wedding and honeymoon and eventually returned to work at the business school. One evening, right before I was about to shut down my desktop computer in my office at Stanford and leave work for the day, I got an email announcing a lecture by a man I had never heard of before. He was going to be talking about something related to banking, but a different sort of banking. He was a banker to the poor. This sounded interesting and, frankly, a little suspicious. Why would the poor need a banker if they didn't have any money? Intrigued, I decided to sit in on the lecture anyway.

The man's name was Dr. Muhammad Yunus. It was the fall of 2003, three years before Yunus and his Grameen Bank would be awarded the Nobel Peace Prize for their work pioneering modern microfinance. But first, on the night I heard him speak, Yunus would change the course of my life.

In 1976, Yunus worked as a professor of economics at the University of Chittagong in Bangladesh. Sometimes he and his students would visit the nearby village of Jobra, where they would conduct surveys and do projects with people living in the poorest households there. Through one of these surveys, Yunus learned just how little money it took to free a group of women—all working as bamboo-furniture makers—from a vicious cycle of predatory lending.

Every day, the women borrowed very small amounts of money (a few dollars' worth) from local moneylenders. The moneylenders set their interest rates extremely high, but the women had no other choice for funding; no one else would lend to them. With their tiny loans, they would buy the materials needed for their day's work, labor furiously to make their bamboo furniture, and sell it at a profit—but sadly, at the end of the day, they would pay nearly all that they had earned in profit back to the moneylenders. Sometimes they'd even owe more than they made, ending up deeper in debt than when they began.

Yunus's survey results showed that for each of these women to break free from this cycle and have the capacity to buy her own materials, it would take only 856 takas, or about $26. Yunus loaned the money to the women himself, interest-free, and collected small repayments every day at a small tea stand in the village. Remarkably, every single woman repaid her debt in full.

Yunus's experiment in that small Bangladeshi village ultimately became the impetus for the establishment of the Grameen Bank, a pioneer in modern microfinance—including not just microcredit (small loans) but other financial products and services for the entrepreneurial poor. Of course, Grameen Bank began with and is best known for its microlending activities, empowering clients to start or grow businesses, invest in their homes, send their kids to school, or simply meet their daily needs. Today the Grameen Bank has over 7.5 million borrowers (more than two-thirds of whom have lifted themselves out of extreme poverty) and has inspired countless other organizations around the world to follow Yunus's lead and serve the financial needs of the poor through microfinance.

Why hadn't other institutions been serving the needs of this group already? Other banks did not want to go to the trouble of doing the paperwork required for such small loans, nor would they take on the risk of accepting borrowers who, like the women Yunus worked with, had no collateral to speak of. Unfortunately, when it comes to traditional banking services, you usually have to have money in order to get money. Thus a large segment of the population—many of whom were women—had been deemed "unbankable" for a very long time, and were shut out of traditional financial institutions.

But Yunus's Grameen Bank and other MFIs like it have turned these traditional ways of thinking completely upside down. They focus on providing access to funding and financial services to the poor because they know that, given the chance, these individuals can be extraordinarily successful clients and responsible borrowers. Worldwide repayment rates for microloan borrowers are upward of 95 percent, and borrowers consistently demonstrate a determination to use the loans to expand their businesses and improve life for their families. The work of these pioneering MFIs has shown that investing in the poor is not only possible and sustainable, it is an effective means to empower people to lift themselves out of poverty.

The night I heard him at Stanford, Yunus talked about microfinance as a movement with the potential to transform the lives of hundreds of millions of people around the world. Yet his story was inspiring to me because it was so accessible: He made it clear that he began his remarkable journey with just a few small steps that anyone could take. Yunus knew all kinds of fancy economic theories inside and out, but the real magic started when he stood up from his desk, traveled to a nearby village, and began interacting directly with the residents there. I pictured him walking around a village in Bangladesh, shaking hands, chatting with people about their lives, asking the right questions, and patiently listening to the answers. Then he took specific actions to address individual needs, reaching into his pocket and lending a few dollars that would have a remarkably powerful impact.

But even beyond sharing an accessible, inspiring narrative of the birth of a world-changing organization, Yunus took my breath away as he spoke about the poor in a way I had never encountered before: as entrepreneurs.

Listening to Yunus speak, I felt genuinely inspired. Not devastated. Not depressed. Not panicked or guilty or defensive. His stories had not been of sadness and suffering, of desperation and hopelessness. These were stories of smart, strong, hardworking people who, with access to the right resources, could become entrepreneurs.

This turned my understanding of poverty on its head. The people Yunus spoke of were not just sad faces on a brochure, synonymous with the issue of poverty itself. They weren't just charity cases or problems to fix, and they weren't just the recipients of endless and unquestioning generosity for the sake of my own moral character development. The environments into which these individuals had been born were the problem, environments that denied them access to the proper tools to thrive. These were not weak, helpless people. These were people who were capable, tenacious, and resourceful. These were people I wanted to be around, not people I wanted to avoid. These were entrepreneurs.

For the first time in a long time, I began to think about the big, overwhelming task of alleviating poverty as something that was actually possible, one person at a time, through a series of small, discrete steps—steps that could be catalyzed with a small loan and support along an entrepreneurial path.

How was it possible that I had heard such different accounts about people living in poverty over the years? Who was telling the more truthful version of the story—Yunus or the nonprofits? I wanted to find out for myself. I wanted to hear more stories, firsthand. Who were these people, really? More important, who could they become?

There was something else. If the people Yunus talked about were really entrepreneurs, people I respected and could relate to, then my role did not have to be that of a faraway observer, or a passive donor, or a scattered volunteer. If their story could be different, so could mine. I could react to them differently. What could my role be now that I knew there was another side to the story?

Who could I become?

Into the Field

After listening to Yunus speak that night, I was inspired to start a new chapter of my own journey. I longed to do something concrete, something meaningful, something specific. I wondered if I could get started the way that he did, simply by spending time listening to the people I wanted to help.

So I decided to try to do what he had done: to connect directly with a few people whom I wanted to serve, and to spend some time listening very carefully to what they needed. I wasn't sure how I would find these people, but I figured others who served the same kinds of folks would have ideas for me. Accordingly, I became a bit of a stalker—not just of Yunus, but of others who I thought could help me learn the things I needed to know to be useful in the microfinance sector. I made a list of microfinance-related organizations in the Bay Area, and then methodically began calling and emailing (or just showing up at the offices of) people in those organizations who I thought could help me.

This is how I came to reach out to a man named Brian Lehnen, the founder and then executive director of Village Enterprise, a nonprofit based in California whose work focused on microenterprise development throughout East Africa. Brian and I met for breakfast at a diner near their main offices in San Mateo, a few miles north of Stanford. From the moment I sat down in the booth across the table from him, I could tell something was going to be different about this meeting. Brian was instantly more approachable than anyone else I had met. He grinned, shook my hand warmly, and asked me to tell him my story. When I placed my résumé on the table between us and readied myself to give an elevator pitch about my skills, my experience, and what kind of internship opportunity I was looking for, Brian cut me off, respectfully moving my résumé aside. He smiled again, folded his hands on the table, looked me in the eyes, and said, simply, "This isn't an interview. Just talk to me. Tell me about who you are and what you're passionate about."

I let it all out. I gabbed away about my desire to help the poor without knowing exactly how. I listed everything I had tried so far and why I felt frustrated by those efforts. I told him about my bittersweet time in Haiti. I told him how I'd expected college to help me figure out what to do but it hadn't quite done the trick. I confessed that I was working in a job for which I was thankful but that wasn't what I wanted to do forever. I explained how I felt stuck, far away from any action on the front lines and far removed from the kinds of people I really wanted to serve.

Then I walked Brian through my experience of hearing Yunus a few weeks earlier, and how I felt convinced I needed to try to do something like what he had done: to meet entrepreneurs, to listen to their stories, and then to respond, perhaps in a new way, based on what they told me. I confessed that I wasn't totally sure that this would be helpful to him or to Village Enterprise, but that I would do something else too if that was a better fit. I insisted I could learn fast and would go anywhere.

Then I finally stopped talking.

The whole time, Brian had been listening. Nodding. He heard me. He understood.

"I think you're right," he said. "You can't really know what the problem of poverty is all about until you go and see it for yourself. You can't know until you are there, really spending time with entrepreneurs. Sounds like it's time for you to get out there."

Brian didn't think I was crazy. He never criticized me for my lack of a specific plan, or questioned whether or not I had the skills or experience to do what I wanted to do. He listened carefully, and reassured me that my instinct was right: The best next step I could take was to get out there, meet real people who needed help, and figure out how to be useful.

At the end of the meeting, I was feeling bold and asked Brian if I could ever reach out to him again with follow-up questions. He offered to meet up for lunch the following week. I was thrilled and accepted the generous invitation before he could change his mind.

We met the next week, and then we met again the following week, and again the week after that. After half a dozen lunchtime conversations, Brian and I had designed a three-month project that would allow me to go to East Africa to interview entrepreneurs Village Enterprise served. My job would be to conduct surveys of the entrepreneurs Village Enterprise funded in villages throughout Kenya, Uganda, and Tanzania. Each entrepreneur I'd meet had received $100 to start or grow their fledgling businesses: repairing shoes, selling spare bicycle parts, growing millet or maize, knitting sweaters, serving rice and beans to workers on lunch break, or countless other enterprising activities. I would spend three and a half months conducting interviews, trying to learn how the grant money had affected their lives.

Before I left for my assignment, Brian and I drew up survey questions for me to use in my conversations with the entrepreneurs. Some of the questions were aimed at simply collecting business-related information, like their revenue, costs, competitors, and the like. But because Village Enterprise's chief concern was alleviating poverty through microenterprise development, most of the survey questions centered on the standard of living of entrepreneurs and their families. These questions aimed to collect data such as whether or not the household's children were in school, how many changes of clothing each family member owned, how many meals they ate each day, whether or not they could afford to eat protein, the quality of their home, what kinds of possessions they owned, and so on.

Brian coached me thoroughly. He spoke to me about culture and customs. He told me about the weather, the language, the food, and gave me advice on what to pack. He prepared me for the extreme generosity and hospitality I was about to encounter. Perhaps most important, he told me stories about his own experiences in the region, ones that illustrated some of the challenges I might face while doing the surveys. He helped me understand what might get lost in translation and why, and how to tease out the most accurate information. For instance, he explained how, despite the best intentions, people might not always answer my questions truthfully. I was a representative of an organization that had provided them with funding and might provide more in the future. An entrepreneur might be tempted to share only positive responses to queries about how much Village Enterprise had helped improve their lives, he warned. Or some might be motivated by pride to demonstrate success and prosperity to a visitor from the United States. Others might just want to be polite and not disappoint a guest in their home. Brian suggested reminding people that there were no wrong answers, and validating every experience they shared with me. He gave me strategies for allowing entrepreneurs to maintain dignity at all times, regardless of how they answered.

Brian suggested warming up the interviewee with small talk and a little information about myself, then starting off with easy questions, asking people their names, their business's name, household demographics, etc. Then I could build up to tougher questions about business operations, revenue, and the quality of their standards of living that might be more difficult to discuss openly without having established a rapport first. To wrap things up and end on a high note, I should ask about an entrepreneur's dreams and aspirations for the future, and whatever other open-ended questions I felt might help me understand their unique story. Brian encouraged me to get to know each individual with a fully open heart, and a willingness to let conversations flow to unexpected places. In fact, he told me, during the unscripted moments people naturally directed the conversation to what mattered most to them.

He taught me so much during those informal training sessions together. He made sure I understood how to ask the right questions. He modeled how to listen carefully and to appreciate the complicated circumstances and psychology of many of Village Enterprise's clients. Most important, Brian took a chance on me and gave me an opportunity that would change my life. He gave me a way to go and see for myself.

A few weeks later I boarded a plane to Nairobi.

Blessing the Shopkeeper

BUILD IN THE MIDDLE OF THE PATH

Between villages outside Dar es Salaam, Tanzania
2005

A few months into my assignment with Village Enterprise, I found myself interviewing (with the help of a translator) the owner of a small shop. The shop was little more than a tiny square room, no larger than a storage closet, with only a few dozen items for sale. The walls were made of used wooden planks held together with rusty nails and covered in a thick, peeling paint, giving the entire structure a look of colorful weariness, like a worn patchwork quilt. The roof was an oddly shaped scrap of aluminum sheeting, riddled with nail holes intentionally clustered together in one spot to allow a small patch of light to creep into the shop. The shop had no particular name. The shopkeeper was called Blessing.

Blessing's little shop was not situated along the side of the road, like all the other kiosks and small shops I had seen in the region. Instead it sat alone, directly in the middle of the well-worn dirt path that led from her village to a nearby trading center, making it impossible to avoid. Villagers traveling between the two points had no choice but to walk past her shop and acknowledge Blessing, who was always there from early in the morning to well past sunset. They might catch a glimpse of the items she displayed on the narrow wooden shelves inside her shop: bars of soap, sugar, cooking oil, kerosene, maize meal, laundry detergent, a few onions and tomatoes, and a variety of other household goods. But Blessing also stocked a number of unusual products in her shop, ones I had not seen in similar village shops throughout my travels in the region. For example, she sold four different kinds of bar soap, instead of just one. She had a package each of AA and AAA batteries. There was lip balm and a relatively high-end bottle of shampoo, both unusual luxuries in the surrounding villages. A jar filled with all sorts of wrapped chocolates and little hard candies sat on the counter, reminding me of a similar jar sitting atop the checkout of the vast supermarket I went to as a kid in my hometown.

Many of the items in Blessing's shop had been unwrapped and repackaged into smaller amounts. Several of the bars of soap were sliced into halves, some into quarters. A few dozen plastic baggies filled with single teaspoons of cooking oil—enough to cook one meal—sat next to larger one-liter jugs. One package of maize meal had been opened and partially emptied, poured into three different-sized cups.

I spent several hours sitting with Blessing just outside her store, drinking chai, learning about her family and her life in her village, and watching her interact with customers who came and went all afternoon. The first customer was a small boy, not tall enough to see over the counter. He stepped lightly onto a large stone that Blessing had placed beneath the counter, and Blessing walked into her shop to greet him. He spoke shyly to her, asking for one of the plastic baggies of cooking oil and a tiny packet of laundry detergent. He handed over a few coins and Blessing handed over his goods. Then he paused for a moment and smiled. Without saying a word, Blessing picked up a small cup with a few dozen pieces of wrapped candy in it, and placed it on the counter before the boy.

He pulled out a piece of candy before whispering a soft thank-you, "Asante," hopping down from the rock, and running away happily.

Several more customers arrived throughout the afternoon, including many more children, all of whom took their piece of candy before leaving the shop. One woman bought the bottle of fancy shampoo, a significant transaction for both Blessing and the customer. Another bought two AA batteries. Others bought some of the more common-looking items, like the soaps and maize meal that were stocked in smaller quantities. Blessing welcomed every customer by name and offered an extended greeting. She usually asked questions while she gathered up the items that the customer needed, and more than once, my translator explained, customers would ask her to pick up a particular product for them the next time she went to nearby Dar to buy goods. Blessing, who could barely read and write, later told me that she would make a mental note of the item named and that she had never yet forgotten a request.

A gifted observer of others, Blessing had found numerous opportunities to fill the needs and wants of her neighbors. Her shop was an aggregation of these insights, and her chosen location in the middle of the path was a response to her realization that the best way to keep understanding her community's needs was frequent interaction: to see as many of her neighbors as she could, and as frequently as possible. Instead of going door-to-door with her wares, which was a long and tiring process, and instead of situating herself farther away from home in the nearby trading center where she might be hidden amid the rest of the vendors, she came up with the unconventional idea to plant herself in the center of that path.

By doing so, Blessing became part of everyone's daily lives in a way that would have made the most seasoned and successful retailer envious. She was, quite literally, in the middle of the action, listening to the people she had chosen to serve, learning of their wants and needs firsthand, and making sure she provided those things every time.

CHAPTER 3

Listen Between the Lines

The Second Valley

"Ready! It is time to go again." Richard Mazengo's voice snapped me back to reality.

The afternoon heat seemed hotter here in the center of Tanzania than anywhere I had ever been, and I had been daydreaming. My mind had wandered into a jumbled reverie, one I had had many times since arriving in Africa. It starred yours truly in a strange sort of wandering mashup of *The Gods Must Be Crazy* and *Le Petit Prince* and other random images of Africa that had found their way into my consciousness over the years from TV and books and a perennial *National Geographic* subscription from my grandparents in Florida. In the daydream, I roamed among squatty baobab trees, wandering across a nameless African desert in classic khaki safari gear (of course). Even though I knew the scene to be a ridiculously stereotyped fantasy of the continent, it kept running through my head.

Now awake, I saw the real thing. At least some of my daydream had been accurate; baobab trees surrounded me, springing up all over the tawny desert where we'd stopped. As I let my eyes adjust to the daylight, I stared into the distance at the horizon, the view rippling from the heat rising off the sand. Words I'd learned somewhere along the way but had never experienced until now lit up in my brain. *Refraction*. *Mirage*. This kind of thing was happening a lot here in Tanzania.

In fact it had begun even before I landed in Nairobi a few weeks earlier. During the final minutes of my flight, I sat wrapped in the hum of the airplane, watching the land pass below, sparkling brown, green, and wet. *Savannah*. Dawn had just emerged and the earth was all soft, round edges. I could see rings of huts, a dozen or so positioned in circles and semicircles; thatched roofs freckled the landscape. *Village*. Footpaths cut through the land, widening in the open fields, then narrowing as they approached clumps of trees. I saw flecks of brown clustered together. *Herd*. They moved slowly in the same direction. *Migration*. There were no clouds in the sky, only drifting gray swirls of smoke that rose from cooking fires below. As the plane continued its descent, I squinted, imagining I could zoom in and see a person. I let myself believe that at least someone down there was looking back up at me, hopeful and welcoming.

It was a few weeks after I had met Blessing, the shopkeeper, in Tanzania. I had made my way from Dar es Salaam to the center of the country to work with Village Enterprise Country Director Richard Mazengo for the final weeks of my assignment. As Tanzania's national director for Village Enterprise, Richard was tasked with taking me to the entrepreneurs I was supposed to interview in the region. We were a few hours outside Dodoma, and so far we were not having the best of luck. Richard had just finished repairing a tire that had gone flat for the third time about an hour earlier. This would happen twice more on the journey back home that night. And, in every case of a flat tire, I was not allowed to help.

Most of the men I met throughout East Africa insisted I just sit and watch as they worked; they believed it was not appropriate for a woman to join them. But even the women I met would not allow me to help because I was a guest. This is not to say that I could do what they did. I couldn't slice a tomato in the palm of my hand with a dull knife. I didn't know how to roll chapati dough as thin as a leaf using an old broom handle for a rolling pin. I'd watch, tense, as they turned pieces of meat on hot cooking stoves using only their fingers, and I'd stare, baffled, as they emerged clean and calm from a dark, smoky, mud-walled cooking hut with a steaming plate of rice and beans. I laughed in disbelief and complete admiration as I watched a woman bake a cake—an actual cake!—in hubcaps balanced upon three rocks over a charcoal fire.

For many reasons, it was difficult to make myself useful, which, unfortunately, was exactly what I was so desperately trying to be.

"Let's go!" I answered back to Richard Mazengo. I stood up from my folding chair in the shade of the fat baobab tree and climbed into the dilapidated pickup. Richard instantly hit the gas. The truck jumped into gear and bumped along, picking up speed. Soon we were careening wildly across the broad Serengeti roadways, tires slipping and skidding and kicking up dust in a thick white cloud behind us, obliterating our view of the path back to Dodoma. The powdery dirt roads, compacted and corrugated from a steady flow of cars on the only main thoroughfare in the area, made steady traction nearly impossible. Still, I relished the speed as it came and went in spurts, the warm breeze on my face, and the sense that at least we were moving toward our destination, a tiny village still a few hours to the east.

I sat on the passenger side of the long bench seat with my arm hanging out the window, the hot wind zipping through my fingers. I tried to keep my gaze fixed on the familiar baobab trees in the distance because if I looked down, I'd be staring through a hole in the floor of the truck where the metal had rusted away and see the blur of the dirt road whizzing by beneath my feet. Clouds of dust billowed into the cab, coating my nose, lips, and throat. When I smiled, the dust stuck to my teeth and made them feel fuzzy. Inevitably, at the end of every day in Dodoma my light skin would be a few shades darker, my brown hair a few shades lighter, and my sweat-soaked T-shirt dulled a yellowish brown, like the desert landscape itself.

Richard sat in the driver's seat with a smile on his face, never looking overheated, always crisp and somehow perpetually dust-free. As we barreled through the desert, he hummed along to a cassette tape of American gospel music from a conference he'd attended in Atlanta several years earlier. He had three cassettes on hand and would take turns popping them into an ancient tape player every time we got into the truck, blasting Jim Reeves, Kenny Rogers, or this current selection, a mix of saccharine-sweet gospel melodies about light and rivers and love. Though I knew the songs would stay stuck in my head for months, I never complained. There was nothing I would change about Richard Mazengo, whose family I lived with during my time in Tanzania, and whose kindness and generosity knew no limits. Richard and I had come to this tiny village outside Dodoma to visit Innocent, one of the many entrepreneurs I would interview for Village Enterprise during my time in East Africa.

I grabbed my camera, notebook, pen, and interview materials and hopped out of the truck. Innocent walked briskly toward us. We smiled and exchanged basic greetings in Swahili—*Habari! Nzuri!*—and began the process of shaking hands, which is not a trifling thing in Tanzania. It is a galvanizing gesture that can last a full minute or maybe many more. After weeks in Tanzania I had learned to extend my right hand but keep my left hand clasped to my right forearm to keep it from getting tired during these long exchanges, shaking and shaking and shaking hands as the conversation unfolded.

Innocent walked us to three handmade wooden folding chairs placed in the patchy shade of yet another gigantic baobab tree before quickly turning around and reentering her house. The chairs were crafted out of crooked but carefully sanded branches and held together with wooden pegs and a handful of precious nails. They were stained with a heavy coat of shiny, tart-smelling, dark brown lacquer, the kind that perpetually feels sticky. When I sat down, the chair reclined steeply; I had to hold my head forward, my chin almost touching my chest, to see my notebook or take notes. I ended up perched on the edge of the chair with my camera and interview materials on my lap, waiting for Innocent to reemerge.

Instead a young girl came out of the small house, holding a pitcher in one hand and a large plastic basin in the other. She walked toward me shyly, knelt, and nodded to a bar of soap sitting in the basin. I reached for the soap as she lifted the pitcher high and slowly poured a trickle of warm water into the basin, creating a sort of faucet and sink. The more she poured, the lighter the pitcher and the heavier the basin became. Her arms shook, one and then the other, struggling under the weight of the shifting water. I tried to wash quickly, though she seemed in no hurry. When the washing was complete, Innocent again emerged from her home with a tray holding two cups of hot chai.

As dusk crept in and the afternoon heat died down, I sipped my tea and listened intently as Innocent told me how with just $100 she had kick-started her business, increased her profits, and made life better for herself and her family.

Sugar in Your Tea

Innocent's business was a simple one: She sold dried maize at a market near her house. That was it. I assumed my interview with her would be just as straightforward. All of my interview questions were guided by the surveys and standard-of-living questionnaire that Brian and I had created before I left California, and at that point I knew them almost by heart.

Before I began asking questions I made note of the things I could see. Innocent's house was a flat-roofed rectangular structure made of packed mud and branches. It was not much bigger than Richard's pickup truck. Maize kernels were spread across the roof, drying in the sun so they could be sold in a nearby market. A thin, gauzy cloth served as a front door. There were small windows with no glass. The ground leading into the house had been carefully swept with a broom, leaving swirls and arcs, almost fingerprint-like patterns, in the dirt. There were old yogurt cups hanging on strings along the front of the house, each filled with dirt, with single tiny green sprouts no more than an inch or two high peeking over the rims. I couldn't help but think of the contrast with the dozen or so heavy hanging baskets that decorated the deck of my parents' house in Pennsylvania, billowing with flowers and ferns, ivy and thick green clumps of moss.

I made quick notes about the state of her home on my survey. I checked a box to indicate that her home was built of packed mud walls, instead of baked brick or concrete blocks. I checked another box noting the thatched roof, not aluminum sheeting. I discretely observed the quality of clothing of the family members. I noted that the children were clothed, not naked, but that all wore badly tattered hand-me-downs.

Then I began my interview. Richard translated.

> ME: *Asante sana* again for taking this time with me. Can you tell me again for this survey, what is your full name?
>
> INNOCENT: My name, it is Mwanga Innocent.
>
> ME: What is your age?
>
> INNOCENT: I am thirty-seven years. Too old! (She laughed.)
>
> ME (looking over and nodding toward the half-dozen wide-eyed kids shyly watching us): Are all of these beautiful *watoto* your children?
>
> INNOCENT (smiles): Yes. They are all mine. So many.
>
> ME: Can you tell me their names and ages, please?

Innocent listed the names and ages of her six children, who ranged from two to eleven years old. The eldest three were girls, one boy was of school age, and the two other tiny ones were not yet old enough to attend school.

> ME: So, four of your children are of school age. Are these children in school?
>
> INNOCENT: Only the oldest boy is. He is eight.
>
> ME: But not the girls.
>
> INNOCENT: No, not the girls.

I wished that I had been surprised at this response, but giving priority to the boys was typical in families that could not afford to send all their children to school.

> ME: Do you plan to send the girls to school in the future?
>
> INNOCENT: Yes, yes, they are next. I cannot afford to yet but we are improving. I will be able to soon.

ME: What other changes have you made already?

INNOCENT: First there is sugar for our tea. This is very good. And then mosquito nets, and . . .

ME: Excuse me for interrupting, but what do you mean about the sugar?

INNOCENT: You can taste it now! It is in your tea. We have sugar now to take with our tea.

ME (taking a sip of tea to show that I got her point): Yes, it's very good. Did you not use sugar in your tea before?

INNOCENT: Only sometimes. Now I can afford this every day. I did this first with the money from the business after Village Enterprise came and gave me the $100. I bought this sugar.

ME: Okay. Can you tell me why you chose to do this first?

INNOCENT: When I have this sugar, I can use it, and also give it to my neighbors. I can invite them into my home and offer them tea. And I can feel proud.

This was the first time I heard about the importance of having sugar in one's tea. It wouldn't be the last. Many other women whose interviews came after Innocent's brought it up as well. This small thing gave Innocent a reason to invite others into her home, and in doing this, she felt connected and important. Sugar in her tea was a gateway to more confidence, strengthened relationships, and eventually greater leadership in her community.

I often think about this small detail because of the crucial lesson it taught me. When I arrived in East Africa, I wanted to learn. I wanted to listen. But I also thought I knew a lot already about what I could do to help the people I was about to meet. If I had been given some sort of magic wand when I had arrived in Kenya just weeks earlier, I would have confidently wielded it, believing I knew how to fix things and improve the lives of the people I so badly wanted to serve. But it didn't take me long to realize that I would have gotten a lot wrong. I would have prioritized things that were not priorities for the people I interviewed. I would have made changes in their lives that were not mine to make.

I needed to learn to value what mattered to *them*. The more I did that, the more useful I could be.

For instance, one family in the middle of a crowded, sprawling slum proudly showed off the padlock they had put on their door. The heavy metal door in its wooden frame was the strongest part of the home; the rest of the structure was made of pieces of wood, branches, discarded pieces of aluminum sheeting, and plastic. But despite the flimsy construction of their home, having a lock for the door made them feel safe and secure. Once I knew to look for details like this, tiny things that may not have made sense to me but that meant something to the people I was meeting, I encountered other examples almost every day. For instance, one woman showed me a clock that did not run, but which she clearly viewed as a beautiful, sophisticated decoration, hanging on her mud wall. Another man proudly pointed to a mattress on the floor; it was the only store-bought furniture in their entire home. His wife and all four of his children slept on it at night while he slept on the floor beside them. Others had used the increased profits from their business activities for valuable services or experiences that I would not have initially guessed, like renting an ox plow for their fields or paying for a bicycle-taxi ride into town for the first time.

Innocent taught me to always let other people decide for themselves what they need to feel empowered, valued, and happy, no matter how surprising their choices. It was tempting to make assumptions about the people I met. The more interviews I did, the more I began to see similarities and common threads among them, especially those who had similar businesses or lived in the same village. It was often difficult to fight the temptation to jump ahead in the survey and fill in the blanks of their stories. But when I resisted the urge, I was often rewarded with answers that I hadn't anticipated. My goal became not only to measure the impact each $100 had made, but to understand what changes each entrepreneur believed had been most significant in their lives. Keeping this perspective front of mind ensured that I was as open as possible to learning what each person I met with had to teach me, one conversation at a time.

And over time, as I listened, I did learn. And I was changed.

The Great Rift

My perspective on poverty, and on the role I could play in alleviating it, was permanently altered by my experience in East Africa. Finally, after so many years of searching, several things became clear about what worked, what didn't, and what that meant for me.

For instance, I saw that just a little bit of business training paired with a small infusion of capital could fuel a motivated individual's climb out of poverty—and that that individual could pull many others along with her. For example, on average, a Village Enterprise grant of $100 directly affected fifteen household members' standard of living. Even beyond this, I saw how the prosperity of one family could affect other families' standards of living, and even inspire change in an entire community.

I observed that no matter how remote the villages that I visited in Kenya, Uganda, and Tanzania, they were relatively well connected to an advanced mobile network. My cell phone worked almost everywhere I went throughout East Africa, even in places far away from an electricity source. I had little trouble keeping in touch with loved ones, and could easily share my experiences—and my new friends—with them. More than once I would offer my phone to an entrepreneur I'd just met when Matt (back in San Francisco) or my parents in Pennsylvania were on the line.

Though it was often slow and intermittent, Internet connectivity also existed in more small towns than I would have ever imagined. Even in villages that were an hour's drive from an Internet café, I would meet people who wanted to exchange email addresses. They may have been able to leave their village only every few weeks to check their inbox, but nevertheless they had the desire and the capability to be connected to the rest of the world.

Maybe most significant of all, I became convinced that, just as Yunus had described, there was a side to the story of the working poor that was not being told. My new friends in East Africa were not defined by their poverty. They were smart, hardworking entrepreneurs. Theirs were not the stories of suffering and despair that I had heard growing up and that had made me feel perpetually guilty. There were, of course, struggles in their lives, but there was also hope, perseverance, and pride. They inspired me.

Notably, not a single entrepreneur I interviewed throughout East Africa asked me for a handout or a donation. They wanted something else: a loan. Why a loan instead of a donation? According to the entrepreneurs I met, they wanted to feel true autonomy and ownership over the businesses they were building. They wanted to do as much as they could by themselves. They wanted to feel independent and strong.

In most of the cases there was no question that a loan would be put to good use. There were obvious, and sometimes enormous, business opportunities all around; it was just a matter of accessing the necessary capital. In one particularly remote village I visited, an entrepreneur pointed out that there was no store selling household goods like soap, cooking oil, kerosene, and the like. Villagers had no choice but to walk several kilometers every day to a neighboring town to buy the simple items they needed. The market clearly existed, and would-be entrepreneurs were ready and willing to meet the demand. All that was missing was capital.

Throughout my time in East Africa, as I shared stories with friends and family back home, overwhelmingly people responded with surprising enthusiasm. Of course, I kept in close touch with Matt as well, and together we began to wonder. . . . What would it look like to help some of these entrepreneurs get the loans they wanted? What if we somehow found the money and loaned it to them ourselves? Would friends and family want to chip in and provide that kind of funding, since it would only be a few hundred dollars? What if we could stay in close touch with the entrepreneurs, documenting their stories, tracking their progress, and cheering them on?

I believed that these inspiring new stories of entrepreneurship were the key to securing loans. It was clear that each story was special— perhaps special enough to inspire a new kind of response in people who had otherwise resigned themselves to helping the poor out of guilt or shame. I knew that it was because of these new stories that the distance and disconnectedness I had felt throughout my life—that great rift between me and the people in the nonprofit brochures and infomercials, whom I had yearned to know and to serve—had begun to close. I wanted others to experience that.

Hear a story about poverty? Feel sad, give a few bucks, and forget about the incident sooner than later.

Hear a story about a hardworking entrepreneur? Feel inspired, lend a few bucks, stay connected, get repaid—and maybe in the end care more than you did before.

By the time I returned home from East Africa I had a clear vision of what I wanted to do. I wanted to create a way for our friends and family to experience these new stories of entrepreneurship. And then I wanted to give them a way to respond differently too—for the first time, not with a donation but with a loan.

Samuel the Goatherd

SEEING IS BELIEVING

Near Kita, Mali
2007

It was late afternoon. The heat of the day slowly dissipated and the air was cool as the gray-gold light of dusk softened everything in view. Samuel sat before me, speaking in a low and gentle voice. His presence seemed to spread a sense of calm over everything around us. The craggy trees looked wispy in the distance. The goats and sheep had called a truce to their scrimmaging and now milled about in the dusty fields. A distant storm rumbled on the horizon.

After a long interview with Samuel earlier that afternoon, I now had the pleasure of simply sitting and talking with him. Samuel's home had been difficult to find, tucked away in a network of small meandering roads and paths far from the main road, which wouldn't have counted as a main road anywhere but Mali. Samuel was a client of a local lending institution that I was reviewing as a potential Kiva partner, and one of the organization's representatives had traveled with me that day so I could observe their work and meet some of their clients. We had arrived in the late afternoon, tired from a journey that had already lasted several hours longer than we had expected. Samuel approached us with a menagerie (goats, sheep, chickens, and others) trailing behind him, like a modern-day Saint Francis.

Samuel told me that he had learned to care for each kind of animal from his father. He had been taught to observe each breed's behavior and preferences. He knew what and how much to feed each animal. He could tell when one was getting sick. He knew what to watch for when the animals were ready to mate, and what to do when a new calf or lamb or kid was being born. Samuel told me story after story about his animals, as groups and as individuals. He had gotten to know each one's personality and peculiarities. He knew which animals were the most mischievous, and which would be first to test out a new fence and try to escape. He knew which were strongest, pushing away the others when he brought them food. He knew which ones would come to him with just a whistle and which were skittish. He took care to keep the peace as best he could among the animals that fought. He could get close to the animals easily, predicting their movements, and could catch a chicken or milk a cow with more grace and speed than anyone I'd ever seen.

In most ways there was nothing unique about Samuel's business. His microenterprise was like many others I have encountered not just in Mali, but throughout Africa, in Ghana, Côte d'Ivoire, Senegal, Morocco, Egypt, Rwanda, and Zambia, and even beyond Africa, in dozens of other countries around the world. Samuel was a simple goatherd, and his business reminded me of other herders, breeders, and farmers I had already met.

I also recognized that Samuel would probably not ever choose to aggressively scale his business, or come up with any notable innovations as he went about his work, or achieve any other traditional benchmarks of success as an entrepreneur. In a conventional sense, Samuel did not have many signs of business success. But there was something special about Samuel himself that drew me in the instant I met him. He had a presence. He looked at the world and saw what was special in it—and he saw what was special in each living thing around him. He was a master of observation, noticing details others would miss. He appreciated those details and found meaning in them, inspiring a sense of wonder and possibility. Because of this, he seemed to be a sort of savant with his animals, gifted at connecting with the creatures under his care. He held a respectful appreciation, almost a reverence, for each of them. This attitude profoundly affected how he treated them, how he talked to me about them, and how well he cared for them.

Let me repeat that. The way he saw them affected how he behaved toward them. To Samuel, each of his animals was a gift from a generous God. Each was precious, meant to be treasured.

Samuel reminded me that our perspective of another living thing will determine how we treat it. If we believe that another person is precious, worthy, and capable, we will believe that their lives are important. We will believe that they have great potential. And our actions will bear this out. If we believe otherwise about the very same individual, if we believe they are insignificant, unworthy, or incapable, our actions will reveal this as well. Sometimes our actions toward another person don't make much of a difference in their lives; other times, we have great power to control or even limit someone else's choices. Directly and indirectly, we create rules, set boundaries, and enforce restrictions for each other. Or we can encourage, give permission, or grant autonomy for another person.

In this way, what we believe about someone else can literally limit what is possible for them, or it can set them free to achieve greatness. Samuel helped me remember this truth, and inspired me to take the extra time and care to notice what is special in the world—and the people—around me.

CHAPTER 4

Don't Ask for Permission—Take It

Legally Impossible

I sat across from the lawyer at an immense polished oak desk. The lawyer had his arms folded tightly across his chest and his eyebrows were raised just slightly, in a way that seemed to question every word coming out of my mouth. I almost wished he would just say what he was thinking and interrupt me with, "You can't be serious. That will never work." At least an outburst like that would have been more efficient.

The lawyer had agreed to give me thirty minutes of his time for $20. It was a special deal the San Francisco Bar Association had going, and we took full advantage of it. He listened as I explained how I wanted to create a way for my friends in the United States to lend money to my friends in Uganda. That's when he stopped me. At *Uganda*.

He whacked his hand down on the desk and almost shouted, "You can't just start lending money over the Internet to other people!" Was I not *aware* of a regulating body called the Securities and Exchange Commission? Had I not *heard* of the Patriot Act? Did I really plan on having each goatherd and each farmer *audited*? He had dozens of these kinds of questions—rhetorical only to him.

After a few minutes of this, he stopped, leaned back in his chair, caught his breath, and said, "Look. I can't help you with this. What you're proposing to do is impossible, legally speaking."

Apparently one person could not just lend money to another person so easily. Especially if the borrower lived in Africa. And especially if the Internet was involved.

Even though my time was not yet up, he stood, so I stood too, and he ushered me out of his office. As I turned to say a final thanks, the lawyer became suddenly paternal, patting me on the back. "Well, good luck." And then just as suddenly, his expression shifted from sympathetic back to serious. "Oh, sorry. I nearly forgot. You can pay the $20 to me directly. Cash is fine."

This was maybe the tenth meeting in a month with a lawyer who had given Matt or me some time, either for free or at a heavily discounted rate. This guy's response was kind in comparison with some of the other reactions we'd gotten. Over a period of a few months, we would end up spending a few hundred dollars on $20 sessions like those.

Our problem was that many lawyers looked at us and saw one thing: risk. Matt and I were young, unproven dreamers who wanted to try something new. Lawyers are trained to see barriers and help people avoid risk, while entrepreneurs train themselves to see possibilities and take smart risks. When a typical lawyer and a typical entrepreneur work together it can result in a clash of cultures.

Finally, over forty lawyers later, we found one lawyer who volunteered to help. Kiran Jain, at the firm Bingham McCutchen, helped us establish Kiva as a 501(c)(3) nonprofit organization, and has continued to champion and serve the organization over the years. She saw something different in us, and believed in the potential of our new, scary idea more than she feared the risks.

Those meetings with lawyers taught us a lot, but not what we had expected. We learned that while it is necessary at times to get experts' opinions, at the end of the day we were the only ones who could make the final call on whether or not to move forward. The lawyers we spoke to correctly pointed out the barriers and potential pitfalls we would face pursuing our idea. Identifying risk was their job. Ours, in turn, was to weigh those risks and find a way through the barriers. It required not only listening to what the lawyers told us but also deciding what to do with that knowledge, just like we'd do with any other advice or opinions. I'm not saying we suddenly became experts in international lending law or money-transmission law or any other legal matters, but we had to learn to use the lawyers' perspectives as a tool, not as the ultimate truth about what was possible in the world.

We had to decide what really mattered to us as we made that choice to move forward. Some people decide to try to avoid risk at all costs. We were not those people. We chose to move forward anyway, knowing we would probably have significant battles to fight along the journey.

Sifting through piles of negative feedback to separate the helpful legal information from the vague cloud of pessimism that some lawyers mixed into their comments took some time. But slowly we found the right questions to ask. The most important one seemed to be: Would a loan to a person in Uganda be categorized as a security (an investment opportunity)? If so, we would need to meet a long list of requirements of the Securities and Exchange Commission (SEC) and take on all of the additional responsibilities and costs of becoming a broker-dealer of securities. We hoped this wasn't the case. But since there was no precedent for person-to-person lending over the Internet, it was very hard to get clear answers from the lawyers we were working with. So we picked up the phone and called the SEC directly to ask them what they thought.

To our surprise, they were responsive and helpful. Their answers to our questions helped us feel confident enough to make crucial decisions about the loans we wanted to provide. The most important piece of information we got through our conversations was this: If we let people lend money to our friends in Uganda at 0 percent interest, the loans would probably not be considered a security, and we could avoid the headache and cost of complying with that long list of SEC regulations. We decided to move forward with a 0 percent loan product.

Sponsor an Entrepreneur

Even before we knew for sure whether or not we were legally in the clear, I began cold-calling bankers, economists, tech gurus, nonprofit leaders, and quite frankly anyone else who would give me the time of day. With every conversation I had about the idea, I got better at communicating our vision, not just because I got better at speaking about it, but because I got better at observing how people were responding to it.

In the first few conversations I ever had about the idea for Kiva, I would cut to the chase and simply explain our idea of letting people in the United States fund microenterprises in East Africa. Didn't that sound like an awesome idea?

What usually happened next: I would spend the rest of the conversation answering questions and trying to clarify what I meant. No, we didn't want people to donate. It would be a loan. Yes, even very poor people could take out a loan. Yes, many actually preferred a loan to a donation. Yes, microlending had been tried before; it had been happening successfully for decades, if not longer. No, a loan would not be tax deductible for the lender; again, we were talking about loans, not tax-deductible donations. No, lenders would not make money when they loaned either, so no, it wasn't an investment. Just a 0 percent loan. No, the loans would not be aggregated in some kind of portfolio; they would be direct, to one person at a time. Yes, I really did think there were individuals out there who would want to lend their hard-earned money, for free, to someone they didn't know. Yes, I really did believe that technology could keep us connected to even seemingly remote areas like rural Uganda. Yes, I agreed that instead of collecting little bits of money from lots of different people to fund one loan at a time, it would be more efficient to just "find some kids who struck it rich, like those Google guys, and get them to donate $10 million all at once," but that was not the point of what we wanted to do.

This would go on and on, and sadly, most people would still leave our conversations confused. Obviously, something about my approach was not working.

I went back to the people who had seemed the most confused, and asked them for their feedback—their most honest feedback. It was hard to hear, but they helped me see that more often than not, I was not matching my language to my audience. In 2004 and 2005, microfinance was not a popular or widely understood concept (this would change in 2006, thanks to Dr. Yunus and his Grameen Bank winning the Nobel Peace Prize), so I needed to stop using words like *microloan* or *microfinance* to anyone outside the industry. Nobody was talking about crowdfunding yet either; it would be years until that became a household term. I had to describe what these things were, and what they looked like, from scratch, to nearly everyone. Many people I spoke with had never been to Africa, or if they had, their experiences were limited to Cape Town or a weeklong luxury safari. So the idea that one could send money to a person in a village somewhere "over there," let alone get it back from that person in a village, was difficult for anyone who had not actually traveled to Africa to imagine. And most people had no conception of how such a small amount of money might be used to help a farmer or a tailor grow her business. I had to walk people through those scenarios too.

Additionally, I learned that while using the right language for each person was the first step, I also had to tell stories to move people from a place of ignorance to a place of understanding. And certain stories were going to be compelling to some people but completely boring to others, so I had to be willing to paint a different picture for each different person.

I tried this new approach, beginning my conversations with something I knew would be familiar to the person I was speaking to. Then I would slowly adjust that picture, one element at a time, until it more closely resembled the vision I was trying to communicate. I had to meet each person where they were, on their side of seeing things, and walk them over to my side, where they could share my vantage point.

For instance, when I spoke to an investment professional, I would say something like this: "As you know, when certain start-ups here in Silicon Valley need funding, they might go to a venture capitalist or an angel investor to get the capital they need. Now, replace the start-up with a seamstress in Cambodia. Instead of an investment size of millions or even thousands of dollars, she only needs hundreds. And instead of coming from a fund, the investment comes from individuals directly. Oh, and instead of investing, individuals just lend the money, at 0 percent interest to the lender. Now put the whole process online." Suddenly, the story of a high-tech entrepreneur pitching rich VCs on Sand Hill Road for millions of dollars—a story they knew well—became a story of a seamstress pitching everyday people for $25. They got it.

When I spoke to tech experts, I would begin with anecdotes about the mobile and Internet connectivity I had had in East Africa. Then I would explain how I wanted to keep in touch with my new friends there: by exchanging not just information, but money as well. Already believers in the power of technology to do all of these things, many techies jumped on board with our assumptions that the Internet could enable all this; at that point they just needed help understanding what a few hundred dollars could do in the hands of a hardworking chicken farmer in Rwanda. They understood.

When I spoke to a general businessperson, I'd asked them to imagine replacing a buyer and seller on eBay with a lender and a borrower. And the product in the middle wouldn't be an old bike or a collection of Star Trek Pez dispensers; it would be as if the borrower was "selling" the opportunity to lend to her.

When I spoke to nonprofit fund-raisers or development officers, I would talk about the power of not relying on just one big check to fund a project, but rather on lots of people putting in small amounts of money, $25 at a time. I also referenced the experience of participating in a child sponsorship program, a well-known initiative to their circles. Instead of sponsoring a child, though, people would sponsor an entrepreneur and would get their "donation" back after a few months.

As I adjusted my language and chose my stories more carefully, the tide began to turn. While the idea for Kiva was not receiving enthusiastic encouragement from anyone at that point, I was not being dismissed or shooed away so aggressively anymore. People seemed at least to understand me, and little by little, reactions changed. Some people even seemed to like what I had to say. My confidence grew.

And then a break came when Matt and I had the opportunity to meet with Geoff Davis, CEO of Unitus, an organization that focused on making large-scale investments in high-growth microfinance institutions. He was someone who knew the relevant landscape. Geoff responded to our request for a fifteen-minute phone call with an offer above and beyond what we would have dreamed: He set aside two hours to discuss our idea in person.

We flew up to Seattle to meet with him, giddy and a little intimidated by the chance to meet a microfinance pioneer we admired so much. Our nervousness melted away within the first few minutes of the meeting. Geoff made us feel comfortable, respected, even important.

We arrived with a one-page description of our idea, and since we were talking to a microfinance expert, we went into detail about how the whole process would work on the ground. We told Geoff how we wanted to build an online platform that would allow people to sponsor an entrepreneur in Africa with an interest-free loan. Would-be lenders could browse profiles of entrepreneurs in need online, lend, and get updates and repayments over time. On the entrepreneur/borrower side, we would partner with existing microfinance institutions (MFIs) to identify entrepreneurs, post their information online, and facilitate the administration of loans. The money for the loans would be raised online from people who could maintain contact with the borrower and receive real-time updates on the progress borrowers were making with their businesses.

Geoff asked us a lot of good, tough questions about how we would establish and maintain partnerships with MFIs. For many of his questions, we had no answers. To help us think through it all, at one point he stood up, walked over to a whiteboard in his office, and began to draw a map of the microfinance landscape. He drew circles and boxes to represent not just the different types of microfinance organizations around the world, but also the organizations that supported those MFIs, and the organizations that funded those organizations, and all sorts of other related groups. He walked us through microfinance consulting groups, microfinance networks, technical service providers, rating agencies, banks, government regulators, and much else. He talked about what motivated each group or organization, what threatened them, and whom they worked with most closely. Geoff's walk-through helped give us a much clearer picture of the purpose, needs, challenges, and incentives driving a variety of organizations that would be relevant to our work in the future. Basically, he drew us a road map of the world we were about to enter and explained how that world worked. It opened our eyes to the vastness of the sector and helped us figure out our place in it.

Leaving Geoff's office a few hours later, we still had a lot to learn about the microfinance landscape and exactly how we'd fit in, but our perspective had been crucially expanded. (Years later, Geoff became one of Kiva's most active board members.)

Hitting Send

Although we had made important progress, by the spring of 2005 Matt and I had hit a wall. It had been nearly a year of countless cold calls, hours of research, business-plan writing attempts, and long conversations and our progress had slowed. We had other things going on as well that seemed to take up more and more of our time. I was patching together work as a consultant with Village Enterprise and a few other nonprofits, and Matt was working a full-time job at TiVo, a pioneering DVR company. We had prepared as much as we could and had reached a point of diminishing returns on all of this so-called preparation. It was time to fish or cut bait.

We chose to fish. So, in the spring of 2005, I found my way back to Uganda to enlist the first crop of entrepreneurs to borrow money on Kiva.

Once again it was a stretch to afford my plane ticket to East Africa, so I patched together two different jobs to fund the round-trip flight. I planned to spend the first week serving as a guide for Village Enterprise, hosting a dozen or so donors, guiding them throughout the region to show them what their donations had helped to accomplish. We would visit a handful of villages in Kenya and Uganda, all of which I had visited the year before. Then I would spend the rest of my time working for another small nonprofit, Project Baobab, that provided grants to high school girls for entrepreneurial projects. Finally, after these two assignments were complete, I would stay on another week so I could return to the village where I had spent a great deal of time the previous year, near Tororo, Uganda, to recruit entrepreneurs for Kiva.

Once I was in Tororo, I sought out our good friend Moses Onyango, a pastor and Village Enterprise volunteer who seemed to be the most connected guy in the community. Moses and I had kept in touch during most of the prior year. He was a savvy, forward-thinking man, eager to explore and connect with the world around him. I knew that once every few days, Moses made his way to an Internet café in town. He was the only person in the village who did so. I brought along a digital camera and asked him to take me to visit some of the people I had met months earlier so that I could learn their stories and understand their current loan needs.

Moses and I ran around rural Uganda with my cheap digital camera, taking photos of our first entrepreneurs, each of whom needed just a few hundred dollars to fund their projects. One of the first visits we made allowed me to reunite with one entrepreneur, Nora Ruhindi, whom I remembered fondly from my last trip to East Africa the year before. I sat with her in her tiny restaurant and was served a generous meal of beans, rice, chapati (a locally made sweet bread), and tea. She told me excitedly how a loan of just $300 would allow her to buy better utensils, plates, and cups for her customers to use, and to purchase some basic building supplies to enlarge her small restaurant. In fact, she was so confident that people would lend her money once they heard her story that she ceremonially gave me a yellow plastic mug—one she used to serve customers—as a souvenir, a symbol of the old things she would be getting rid of as soon as she got her loan. I still have it today. I also returned to the home of Katherine, the fishmonger, who now needed $500 to increase her stock and open a new location closer to Tororo town. I sat down with Eunice Alupo, who needed $300 for her used-clothing business. Betty Obote needed $500 to buy cows and open a butcher shop. Emmanuel Ahabwe needed $500 to expand his produce stand. Apollo Kutesa, a goatherd, needed $500 to buy more goats. Rose Mbire needed $500 for her produce business. These seven entrepreneurs were Kiva's first.

After visiting all of them and collecting the information we needed, Moses and I headed to the local Internet café and sat down at a clunky old desktop computer, covered with dust and slow as a tortoise. There, silently cursing the dial-up connection, we painstakingly uploaded seven entrepreneurs' photos, along with their stories and loan needs, on a bare-bones website Matt had built over the previous weeks at www.kiva.org.

The next day, I left my digital camera with Moses, hugged him good-bye, and boarded a plane back to San Francisco. As soon as I got home, I drafted an email to friends and family, telling them about the website and our little project. We couldn't promise repayment. We couldn't promise much of anything. But we hoped they would want to join us in this experiment to lend $25 to seven friends on the other side of the planet.

We hit send and held our breath.

Leila and Zica the Hairdressers

BET ON YOURSELF

Rio de Janeiro, Brazil
2008

I could tell you how my day in Rio began, or I could tell you how it came to a close: As the sun set, I found myself in a loud, lively dance party in the middle of an otherwise quiet neighborhood, surrounded by dozens of employees of Beleza Natural. They moved and sang and laughed and hugged and clapped and shouted and sweated. The women formed a circle, and I joined in on the edge of the ring, until Leila Velez—one of Beleza's co-founders and CEO—grabbed my hand and pulled me into the center. Even though we had just met a few hours earlier, I smiled and went with the flow. Her enthusiasm was contagious. I let go and danced!

Celebrations like this were a regular occurrence for this group of women, who all worked together. I had the privilege of joining in on the fun when I went to Brazil in 2008 on assignment for the Stanford GSB to write a case study on this incredible start-up with a real-life rags-to-riches story.

Beleza's story originates with Leila's co-founder, Heloísa Assis, or "Zica." One of thirteen children in a very poor family, Zica grew up in a favela, one of the many slums on the outskirts of Rio de Janiero. Constantly surrounded by siblings, she learned early on how to make sure her voice was heard among many. Even as a small child, she had a determined, independent streak.

Zica began working at an early age to help with the household income. She began with domestic jobs—as a nanny, a maid, and a housekeeper. Later, she moved from domestic work to spend a few years as a sales assistant. However, she knew that she hadn't found her true passion in any of these jobs. This all changed when she began to work as a hairdresser.

In the world of hairdressing, Zica felt alive and happy. She easily connected with her clients, women who came to her in order to feel confident, beautiful, and hopeful. The opportunity to make sure they felt better about themselves by the time they left the salon was, to Zica, the entire point of the interaction. The haircut or new style she gave them was just one way to make sure this happened.

As Zica served her clients, she began to realize that most products offered by salons were not designed for women with tightly curled or frizzy hair. Even though the vast majority of Brazilian women's hair has this kind of texture, the best products had only minimal effectiveness. Much to her frustration, she was consistently unable to provide her clients with the results they desired: smoother, more relaxed hair. Zica told me that her clients felt unimportant or even at fault in some way because "nothing worked on their hair." Additionally, the women with the toughest hair to work with were Afro-Brazilian or of mixed race, among the poorer minority groups in Brazil. They often lived far from the wealthier city center and had to spend more money on a long journey to the salon. They could not afford to come frequently, so each ineffective visit was that much more disappointing.

Zica became passionate about solving this problem. She decided she would try to create a product that would work for the kind of kinky, tightly curled hair she kept encountering in the salon. For ten years, she worked with her husband, Jair, researching formulas to treat curly hair, and mixing chemicals to try to improve them. Zica had no training in chemistry but she kept at it, and after years of trial and error, research, and feedback from countless clients, she created her first product, a hair relaxer called "Super-Relaxante." To get help marketing and selling her product, Zica and Jair reached out to her sister-in-law Leila, and Leila's husband, Rogerio Assis, for assistance.

Together, the four opened the first Beleza Natural salon in 1993. Beleza Natural translates to "natural beauty," because Zica and Leila firmly believe that every woman is beautiful whether or not she has been able to afford to come to a salon—and that a salon experience should not override but merely reveal each person's inherent natural beauty. Their core mission is "to offer solutions, through products and services, for beautiful and healthy hair, while at the same time promoting self-esteem." All that Beleza does is in the spirit of helping women to see and believe in the beauty they already possess.

Word of Zica's salon, her remarkable products, and her special hair-treatment process spread like wildfire. Within a few months, her humble salon in the Tijuca district in Rio de Janeiro was attracting more clients than it could handle. The small team worked overtime to try to meet demand, but it was clear from the start that Zica had hit upon something big.

Beleza Natural expanded quickly and became hugely popular. The Super-Relaxante formula Zica created was not the only innovation that set Beleza apart. Early on, Leila and Rogerio came up with an equally innovative salon experience. Both former McDonald's employees, they decided to provide a salon experience that utilized the best of the assembly-line process they had seen in the restaurant. They imagined a client moving through the salon, going from one station to the next to the next, working with a number of specialists along the way; today, their seven-step process is one of the most beloved parts of the Beleza salon experience. One staff member greets a client; one collects her payment; one makes sure the client is seated comfortably as she waits for service; another may do a consultation with the client; another prepares the client's hair for the application of the first round of products; and so on. Clients get to see many people who respect and validate them and even make them feel they are part of a community. The level of service Beleza Natural salons provide, particularly to the market segment they serve, is unmatched.

Demand for Super-Relaxante skyrocketed, and it is now patented in Brazil and manufactured locally in the company's own factory, along with a full product line under the same brand name. Additionally, the company established a prestigious training center for all its professionals. The Technical Development Center was inaugurated in 1999 and offers programs for employees to learn the company's mission, vision, and values, as well as the exclusive techniques Beleza Natural is known for. Every new employee is required to complete at least one course in behavioral, technical, or management education. For many newcomers, working at Beleza Natural is the first opportunity for employment they have ever had, as the company even welcomes those who have finished only middle school.

Beleza Natural uniquely benefited from the cross-pollination of four diverse co-founders, and in particular, from the leadership of Leila and Zica, who have become role models for many other aspiring women entrepreneurs. Both women are widely recognized as powerful and influential leaders across the country and the world. Leila was Endeavor's "Female Entrepreneur of the Year" in 2011, and *Forbes* named Zica one of the top ten most powerful women in Brazil in 2013. The company continues to grow rapidly, and recently received a $35-million-dollar investment to enable expansion to 120 stores. These stores will employ 15,000 employees and serve millions of customers each year, and should earn $500 million in revenue by 2018.

While Leila and Zica's entrepreneurial journey can teach many lessons—about partnership, about innovation, about focusing on an underserved market, and much else—above all, to me their story is about confidence. Their products empower women by making them feel more beautiful. Their salon experience is designed to make clients feel special and important. Every staff member is respected, honored, and celebrated.

Zica and Leila believed in themselves even when, on paper, they had none of the formal education one might think was necessary for their journey. They didn't hold degrees in chemistry that helped them run their laboratories and concoct the patented products they're so famous for. They didn't have formal instruction as educators with specialized knowledge that helped them design training programs for their employees. They did not go to business school to prepare themselves to build the empire that Beleza Natural has become. Zica and Leila, a former maid and an ex-McDonald's employee, knew they had within themselves all they needed to begin their journey. They did not wait for another person or institution to declare them ready or grant them permission to pursue their dreams. They knew they needed no one's approval but their own.

CHAPTER 5

Embrace the Rough Edges

Unproven

In a 2007 blog post, Guy Kawasaki, a well-known tech evangelist, wrote about some of the most striking lessons he learned from the Kiva story. In this particular post, entitled "Bank on Unproven People," he writes, "What would the ideal background be of the founder of Kiva? Investment banker from Goldman Sachs? Vice president of the World Bank? Vice president of the Peace Corps? Vice president of the Rockefeller Foundation? Partner at McKinsey? How about temporary administrative assistant at the Stanford Business School? Because that's how Jessica started her quest."

It's true; back then, I had had none of the titles or qualifications that I thought (at the time) a great entrepreneur ought to have before launching something of her own. And for most of my life this never bothered me. It never occurred to me that I needed much to pursue and accomplish whatever I wanted to do.

But then I started working at Stanford, and I began to compare myself with all of the amazing students that I interacted with each day. Many had degrees from top-ranked undergraduate universities. Nearly all of them seemed to have done more than one truly extraordinary thing, with stories of Everest expeditions, prestigious awards, jaw-dropping artistic endeavors, new records set in one thing or another, and countless other feats. Some had founded successful organizations before they got to Stanford; others would go on to do so right after they graduated. I admired those students so much, and kept coming back to the one thing they had in common: the MBA program. Clearly, they thought this was the best next step in their conquests. So, I put them—and the Stanford MBA program—up on a pedestal, imagining GSB graduates had powers to see and do things that I could never do myself without going through the program too. I would think to myself, "If only I was a student here and knew what they knew, then I would be ready to do something truly amazing. . . ."

I said this to myself so many times that eventually I decided to take the plunge and begin the process of applying. I realize now how naïve my thinking was when I first decided to apply. I wasn't exactly sure what the MBA degree would suddenly help me do in a practical sense that I couldn't do already; I just believed if I could only add those three little letters to my résumé, extraordinary things would start happening for me.

This was all going through my mind just a few months after I heard Dr. Yunus speak, in the late fall of 2003. I was already cold-calling microfinance organizations and begging for a chance to work with them. I finished my Stanford application along with a handful of others (for schools I was significantly less enthusiastic about), and turned in all the paperwork just before leaving for East Africa with Village Enterprise. A few weeks into my work with Village Enterprise, fully immersed in the experience, I stopped at an Internet café in Tororo to check my email. When I saw an official message from the Stanford Graduate School of Business, a wave of anticipation washed over me.

As the email loaded incredibly slowly on the dial-up connection, I began to panic. What if I got in? What if I didn't? What would I do? What was next for me?

In response to my own question, a clear thought flashed in my mind: "It doesn't matter." It wasn't an apathetic, who-cares-anyway sort of "it doesn't matter." Instead, it was a reminder to let go of what I couldn't control, and to remember that what would come next in my life was up to me. I might not be able to choose to get into a particular school, but I could choose the work that I wanted to do.

Maybe those thoughts were a defense mechanism, or maybe they were divine inspiration. Either way, the clarity was impossible to ignore. I had spent the previous weeks surrounded by local entrepreneurs who had decided to take matters into their own hands and build better lives for themselves. If Patrick the brickmaker could build a thriving business using literally nothing but the dirt beneath his feet, who was I to pause in the pursuit of my dreams if Stanford rejected me? If the farmers and seamstresses and bakers and vegetable sellers I had met had made such progress in their lives without even a secondary-school education, why should I wait for a stamp of approval from some MBA program to begin **doing the things I really wanted to do in the world? No one, not even my** dream school, could decide my future but me. So then. *What was next?*

Suddenly I knew without a doubt that I was the only one who got to answer that question. Whether or not others agreed that I was experienced or qualified or smart enough, I would forever limit myself if I let my actions hinge on the approval of anyone else—whether a director of admissions, some potential future employer, or any well-intentioned naysayer for that matter. There I was in East Africa, right in the middle of the greatest adventure of my life, feeling more inspired than I had ever been. The whole world was before me. *What was next?*

The email finally opened and in a split second my eyes found the word "unfortunately" in the first few lines of text. There it was, right in front of me: the challenge I had been dreading. Could I make things happen on my own, or did I need someone else's permission to start? *What was next?*

I deleted the email, got up, and went back outside to continue my work for the day. The next day, I dove into the work that I loved again. I kept doing that, day after day. And I had a few of the most incredible months of my life.

Almost exactly a year later that work led me to return to the same horribly slow computer at the same dusty Internet café in Tororo. While I was awaiting a response from the Stanford GSB again—I had decided to apply a second time, this time with a very different perspective—when I checked my email that day, my inbox held no news about my application. But that wasn't the reason I had come to the Internet café. I was there with my digital camera and a host of photos and bios of the very first borrowers to upload onto Kiva's beta site.

Days later, after I returned home to San Francisco, I still had not received an email from the Stanford GSB. Instead, one afternoon my phone rang. It was Derrick Bolton, the GSB's director of admissions. Every applicant knows what a call from Derrick means. I had been accepted to the class of 2007.

I can say without a doubt that the education I received at the Stanford GSB was instrumental in Kiva's success and in all that I have done since. I cannot say enough good things about my alma mater, its leadership, the alumni community, and all that the program stands for. But my MBA wasn't what launched Kiva. In fact, had I gotten accepted to the program the first time around as a member of the class of 2006, I would have missed the opportunity to learn an important lesson about stepping up and not waiting for anyone else's approval to pursue my dreams. And, let's be honest, I would have been too busy studying to have launched Kiva.

No amount of education will necessarily make you feel that you are ready to start something new. Even after I got my MBA, I found myself wishing I had more specific knowledge about microfinance. Later, once I felt intelligent enough about microfinance, I was convinced I needed more expertise in finance. Then it was more management experience. Then I was sure I needed to learn how to code. The list goes on. We can always tell ourselves we need just one more thing, one more experience, before we are ready. But more often than not, we are ready right now, just as we are.

Year One

Let's go back to the moment when Matt and I sent that very first email to a few dozen friends and family members, asking them to lend a total of $3,500 to those initial seven entrepreneurs. We hit send and waited.

We didn't have to wait very long. The money came in virtually overnight. We promptly sent it along to Moses, who served as our first ad hoc loan officer, in Uganda. He then loaned it out to each entrepreneur.

As the following few weeks unfolded, Moses sent frequent updates covering not just business growth and loan-repayment progress, but also colorful details about the entrepreneurs' daily lives. He wrote about how the rainy season affected someone's mud hut, and why the trading center was busier than usual that day, and what exactly a family ate for a big Easter dinner celebration in rural Uganda. The updates became topics for discussion with our friends and family, our first lenders, who felt increasingly attached to the entrepreneurs they had funded.

A few months later I started my first classes at the Stanford GSB, and Kiva's first loans were repaid. For Katherine, the fishmonger, her $500 loan allowed her to sell more varieties of fish and, in her words, to "take my children to school, buy two cows and five goats, and open a savings account." Her business alone supported eleven individuals. It was clear that our experiment, though tiny, was already having an impact on real people.

It was mid-October 2005. I called Moses and asked him if he would be up for helping us find more borrowers to post on the site. Over the next few days, I worked with him to upload the next round of borrower profiles, and again I reached out to friends and family. We also took the word "beta" off the website and declared ourselves official, posting a brief press release on the site that our friend Krista Van Lewen had written for us. Kiva had launched!

And at first nothing happened. The same few dozen friends and family members faithfully visited the website, and the new loans got funded by more or less the same lenders who had loaned to the previous entrepreneurs. But within a few weeks things began to change.

In early November a handful of blogs wrote about our project. Then a few more did. Then hundreds. By mid-November, two very popular blogs, Daily Kos and Boing Boing, featured Kiva, and the resulting traffic to our website obliterated our supply of loans in just a few hours. We scrambled to design a splash page explaining the deficit, and called Moses in the middle of the night to see if he could find more entrepreneurs right away.

The initial onslaught of buzz from the blogosphere was quickly followed by mainstream press coverage, from *The Wall Street Journal* to CNN, the BBC, ABC, and NPR. When Muhammad Yunus, the original inspiration for my desire to pursue work in microfinance, won the Nobel Peace Prize months later, we were mentioned in articles alongside him.

The following months brought an ongoing series of waves of support from people all over the world. Well-respected leaders in the tech and nonprofit sectors, some of whom had been inaccessible to us just a few months earlier, began to follow and praise Kiva's efforts. Our application to become a 501(c)(3) nonprofit was finally approved. LinkedIn founder Reid Hoffman joined our board.

One year after our launch, PBS's *Frontline/World* aired a fifteen-minute documentary about Kiva, driving so much traffic to the website that it crashed for three days. Once it was back up, $250,000 was loaned in a week. (To put this in perspective, we had raised barely $500,000 in the entire previous year.) And within the next month we had raised a million dollars.

When Chaos Works

As Kiva crossed that million-dollar threshold, I remember marveling at how much had happened in such a short time. I also remember laughing to myself because, well, in some ways it was hard to believe that the whole thing hadn't imploded. As hard as Matt and I had worked, things had been messy. But we were not embarrassed by our chaotic beginnings. In fact, we loved our humble, scrappy first year. We felt proud that we had figured out ways to make it through, despite all we lacked.

For instance, for the first round of loans, we hadn't yet built a way for the website to process payments online. (People like my grandmother who didn't use computers but still wanted to participate just handed me a few $20 bills and told me to lend it to someone.) Our logo, the one still used today, was designed by a friend we couldn't afford to pay, so we bartered, giving him an old guitar for the work. When our Internet service went down—or, should I say, when the Internet we were "borrowing" from our neighbors went down—we would head to a local donut shop that had free Wi-Fi and was open twenty-four hours a day to finish our work before sunrise. Since we couldn't afford to compensate any staff early on, we begged our friends who worked at big tech companies in Silicon Valley to help us piece together the website during their weekends and bought them pizza as payment instead. In fact, none of our earliest staff had salaries for months or more; for better or worse, I didn't take one for over two years. Somehow we made it work.

In the beginning of any venture, there will be rough edges. Kiva's situation was not unique; the early days of many start-ups are not that glamorous. You probably won't have everything you think you need. And you certainly won't know everything you need to know, like what is going to happen next. Nobody can see into the future or map out everything in advance. Most days, you just have to show up and begin, be willing to learn as you go, and take steps forward with whatever resources you have (or don't have).

Don't be embarrassed by your first drafts, first steps, or first anythings. As Steven Pressfield reminds us in his inspirational book *Do The Work*, messy beginnings are natural. "Babies are born in blood and chaos; stars and galaxies come into being amid the release of massive primordial cataclysms." Everything big once started small, and those small beginnings often unfold in disorder. Don't be afraid of this disarray. It's okay. Actually, it's more than okay. It means you have really begun, and are pushing yourself to learn and grow. If it feels like you're moving just a little bit faster than is comfortable, you're probably going at the perfect pace.

As you figure it all out, don't fall into the trap of comparing yourself with others. In Kiva's earliest months, had we compared our pilot round of loans of only seven borrowers and $3,500 to any other online marketplace or platform, or any microfinance institution, we would have felt small and insignificant. We would have gotten discouraged. Had we compared our long list of unanswered questions and unproven hypotheses to a business school case study of any large, successful organization, we might have felt foolish. We only knew a few things to be true. We were testing everything else. It was a hectic time of experimentation and hustle and risk-taking—and that was just as it should have been at that stage.

Zica and Leila began in their own kitchens, concocting hair products from scratch. They didn't stop when their work got messy and chaotic, or when their initial mixtures failed. Patrick, the brickmaker, did the same. He grabbed what was in front of him and started shaping, literally, his idea into reality. He figured it out, making mud into brick, one handful at a time. Whenever you are stuck or don't know how to begin, remember these entrepreneurs. Grab whatever resource you have in front of you and start shaping. Start defining. Force yourself to take one concrete step, any step at all, toward making the thing you want to do a reality.

Just about anything you can do today is better than doing nothing, and you'll be able to do even more tomorrow if you begin with something today. When it's messy and imperfect, embrace it. Roll up your sleeves, get your hands dirty, and start.

Constance the Farmer

BE THE BANANAS

West of Nairobi, Kenya
2004

I met Constance on a sweltering afternoon in April, in southern Kenya. I was sweating through my clothes—a dusty purple T-shirt and drab yoga pants—but Constance glowed. She was pristine, dressed in a bright *kanga* with a matching head wrap and skirt. But the bright colors weren't what made her stand out: Her confidence did. She exuded it. In fact, she was a little bit arrogant! And I loved it. What a refreshing, uplifting contrast to some of the women I had met who stood with their heads slightly bowed, avoiding eye contact and speaking just above a whisper. When I met Constance she immediately grabbed my hand with both of hers, squeezed tight, and shook vigorously as she looked me straight in the eyes. She spoke so energetically she was almost shouting. And you could tell that she thought everything that came out of her mouth was correct, if not inspired. Right before saying something she believed to be especially clever, one side of her mouth turned up and a dimple appeared, like she knew a secret. She would clear her throat and hold her finger straight up and shake it quickly, and then she would finally speak.

Constance had lots of children. As we spoke, they were running around too quickly to be counted, except for the three staring at me wide-eyed from the doorway of her home of mud and branches. The children had the familiar smiles of their mother, but not yet her confidence. They looked at me and whispered to one another, and when I made even a small gesture of recognition at their stares—with just a wink or a nod—they burst into giggles and ducked back inside. When Constance called them over to greet me, all chaos stopped and they approached, suddenly serious and shy. They each held out a small hand while they stared down and whispered the only English they knew, "Hallo howawyou," and with a quick tiny handshake they giggled again and jumped away.

Constance had always lived here, she said, and her family before her had always lived here too. This was their land. It was theirs not because of any deed or papers. When I asked about her legal land ownership, which I'd wondered about because there were no men in the household and a woman owning land was so rare, Constance gave me a gentle, scolding smile and shook a slender finger at me. She explained that it was her land because her family lived there now, and had lived there always, and would never leave. What else could it mean to own something? She could not imagine. Generation after generation of people in her family had come from, lived off, and returned to this very patch of earth outside her hut. A line of large rocks in the yard on the side of her home marked the graves of many of these ancestors and relatives, including Constance's husband. This was her land.

She knew the land intimately. She knew every rock and every clay deposit. She knew where the rainwater would run, and knew where to dig shallow ditches or pile up mounds of dirt to redirect the rivulets of precious water. She described how the slope of her land affected runoff and erosion, even though she didn't use those exact words. Constance knew her land so well that she could account for its deficiencies too. She had observed it under a variety of conditions, saw it change through each season, and knew how it would respond to her nurturing interventions.

Constance talked to me at length about the importance of the banana trees and the eucalyptus trees on her land. She was particularly proud of the bananas, the main thing she sold. Once in a while, she sold some of the cassava too (most of the other crops were for her and her family to eat), but she kept focusing on her bananas. She insisted her bananas were the best, that she had the most banana trees of any of her neighbors.

Apparently, those neighbors agreed. Constance worked informally with a group of other farmers who lived nearby to pool ideas and coordinate crops. The group gathered to discuss how business was going, to share best practices, to discuss market trends, and much else. Some had attended training sessions at a local microfinance institution and had taught Constance what they had learned about a variety of topics, from irrigation strategies to hybrid seeds to natural fertilizers. Constance was proud to have passed along her own knowledge too, and explained how she had once taught the group to plant in rows and evenly space the plants, rather than scattering the seeds around randomly.

Technically, the group members competed with one another, selling to the same customers in the same main market. But Constance told me that they had talked openly about this early on, and that she had made sure they all came to an agreement to cooperate. Constance had convinced the group to "make room for each other" in the market, each of them focused on selling only certain items. Each person had suggested what they wanted to sell, and then Constance led the group to reach agreement on who sold what. While no one was forced to do this, they respected each other and knew that everyone would gain more in the end if they just planned a little. Instead of seeing specialization as a sacrifice, they all, according to Constance, felt happy to know they would be given space to focus on something distinct. Standing on her patch of land, Constance listed the things her neighbors grew. Pointing to those neighboring farms, she said, "She is the cassava, and he is the maize, and they are the millet . . ." and so on. And then she raised her eyebrows and smiled an even bigger smile, and in a grand conclusion she announced, "And I am the bananas."

Being the bananas was a big deal. Bananas can be harvested year-round, so she had a staple crop to sell in every season. Some of her banana trees were already over a decade old and required very little upkeep. And most important, everyone in her village ate bananas, and despite the fact that many families had their own banana trees, there was still demand for more; so the banana market was as big as it got. She had asserted herself and established her role as the gatekeeper among her peers of an important, popular, resilient, easy-to-maintain crop. It was a huge coup. Constance had hit the jackpot.

Now, did other people come to the local market from other villages, also selling bananas? Sure. Constance couldn't stop that from happening. But she had made her decision, chosen her mission, fought for it, and she stuck to it. She felt a responsibility to the others from her own village who had let her take the lead with that crop, so she stayed strong, committed, and confident. This confidence—the confidence that had helped her secure her spot as the main seller of bananas among her village group in the first place—also helped her establish herself as a leader at the market, even among the other banana sellers. She had carved out a niche for herself, and she thrived. Anyway, nobody's bananas were better than Constance's (at least according to Constance).

I am inspired by Constance's approach to her own mission and to her competition. She knew who she wanted to be, but didn't ignore the others around her. She stepped up, gathered her competitors together, learned from them—and let them learn from her—and then claimed her territory.

CHAPTER 6

Decide Who You Will Be

My Dad's Mission

It was the summer of 1992, a few months before I would start high school. Dad and I sat in the family car, parked in our driveway, with the windows down to let in the warm breeze. I sat on the passenger side; my legs were stretched out, feet on the dashboard. Dad sat in the driver's seat, reclined a bit, with his hands behind his head.

The car was where we went to have long talks. This was our special place together. Whether we ever drove anywhere or not, there was something about sitting side by side and staring out the front windshield at the horizon that got us talking about anything and everything.

"So, how are you feeling about the move?" he asked.

Since I was two years old we had lived in the same house in a suburb outside Pittsburgh, Pennsylvania. I was now in eighth grade, and in a week I would be finishing up the semester. On the last day of school, while my brother and I were in class, our entire house would get packed up and put into a moving truck to be driven thirty minutes away to our new neighborhood. It was a short move, just to the other side of town, but it felt like I would be a world away from everything I had known.

"I guess I'm feeling okay. It's going to be weird to have to start from scratch at a new school and make new friends."

"You know, Jess, you're going to do great. Just keep being yourself and everyone will love you, like everyone always does," he said matter-of-factly. Neither of my parents held any bias about the subject of my likability, of course.

"Yeah. I guess so."

"You're gonna do great. Just ..." and then, in a silly voice, "... remember who you are!"

I sighed. "Dad, are you quoting Rafiki from *The Lion King*?"

He laughed and admitted that, yes, he was indeed quoting the wise little mandrill from the Disney story. But he got serious again, and went on. "Actually I was just listening to one of my business books on tape and it was saying the exact same thing, just in more complicated language. The basic idea is ..." And with that Dad excitedly began to summarize one of his latest inspirations. I smiled. That's my dad.

Dad reads a lot of business books, and even when I was a kid his advice to me would often be peppered with ideas from one author or another. What would Stephen Covey say about balancing homework and extracurricular commitments? How would Dale Carnegie deal with the mean girls at school? What tips would Anthony Robbins (Dad would call him Tony, like they were close buddies) give me before I had to speak in front of my whole class? I was as familiar with the names of these gurus as I was with the characters and stories in my *Illustrated Classics* or *Baby-Sitters Club* collections. It wasn't until much later that I discovered that not all dads and daughters talk about Lee Iacocca and *The E-Myth*.

Thanks to my dad, I've known what a mission statement is for as long as I can remember. I know now that that was no accident. The motivating conversations we so often had seemed spontaneous and natural whenever they happened, but I now see how much thought he put into the timing of those moments. (As a parent myself now, I look forward to copying some of his techniques when my kids are old enough.) For instance, every summer, Dad and I had a ritual of sitting down and discussing the coming school year. To commemorate the start of a new grade, we would choose a theme for the academic year. In eighth grade, the theme was "Keep Your Head," a mantra for avoiding the hazards of peer pressure. In my junior year of high school, as I was immersed in answering college application questions, we chose the counterintuitive "Ask the Right Questions" to remind me to think proactively and explore all avenues as I navigated the many options for my future. I didn't know it at the time, but these were like mission statement warmup exercises. They taught me to approach different projects and seasons of my life with intention and purpose.

The power and importance of having a solid and clear sense of identity, and designing the right mission statement that stems from that strong foundation—for a business, a venture, an adventure, a particular year, or even for a life—was probably the most important thing my dad learned from all those business books he read. Throughout my childhood, and even when I left for college, he would repeatedly remind me of the importance of reflecting on my purpose, and creating and sticking to corresponding goals that would help me stay on the course I wanted for my life. He urged me to use my own mission, and not the choices or expectations of others, as a beacon. What was important in life, he insisted, was not how I measured up to anyone else—it was how I measured up to the aspirations I had for myself.

My mission statement for my career has been a constant work in progress, but for quite a while now it has been this: to love others and inspire hope by championing the entrepreneurial spirit that exists in all of us. Through Kiva and other ventures, I have aimed to manifest this by connecting entrepreneurs with the resources and community they need to succeed. Having this mission has allowed me to make decisions about where and how to spend my time, and has helped me to see (and to articulate to others) how all of my work—whether full-time or part-time, ongoing or project-based, paid or unpaid—fits together as a cohesive whole.

So when we first dreamed about what Kiva could be, crafting a clear mission statement that laid out our values and vision became a hugely important step in defining our identity as an organization. Over the summer of 2005, we spent weeks working on the language and ideas we wanted to express. Finally we came up with this simple statement of purpose for Kiva: to connect people through lending to alleviate poverty.

Simple as this statement may seem, it is actually packed with meaning and significance. It defines the "what," "how," and "why" of our organization. The "what" is to connect people: Everything hinges on Kiva's ability to draw people closer to one another across any border or boundary. The "how" is through loans: We believe that lending, rather than donating, provides a powerful, sticky tool for connectivity and impact. The "why" is, of course, for poverty alleviation: This is the motivation for our work, and the catalyst for creating Kiva in the first place.

That mission statement has defined Kiva's first decade and helped set it apart from thousands of other microfinance-related organizations. That mission statement helped clarify that, for instance, Kiva did not exist only to raise money in any way possible for other great lending organizations to put to use, or simply to become a big, powerful network of microfinance institutions. Our mission has focused on connecting people, one at a time, through the act of lending, for the purpose of poverty alleviation. That mission has served to focus and direct the Kiva team over the years, and I believe it is a crucial part of what has allowed the organization to know when it is succeeding and when it is off track or losing sight of what matters most.

Letting Ten Million Go

Sometimes an organization's toughest competition is some other possible version of itself—the other path that your venture could take if it had slightly different priorities. Fight the temptation to drift off course in pursuit of other opportunities that might objectively be good opportunities, but that have little to do with what is most important to you. Beware of mission drift: making a series of choices that slowly pull you away from the path you've chosen. That alternative path may not lead to obvious disaster at first, but if it is not in line with your mission, you may fall short of your full potential.

A year and a half or so after Kiva's launch, we had our first (but not our last) big moment of temptation to drift away from our chosen mission. Our small team was crammed into our one-room office when the phone rang. I was closest to a phone, and since we only had one line—which served as our customer-service line, our media-relations line, our press line, and everything else—I picked it up not having the slightest idea who it might be. The voice on the other end of the phone was that of the director of a new, very well funded corporate social responsibility initiative for a well-known tech company.

He excitedly introduced himself and dove into the reason for his call. "What Kiva's doing is just fantastic," he said. "We want to help. And we have $10 million to put into your project."

I was speechless. Ten million dollars was just about as much as we had raised up until that moment in the entire year and a half of Kiva's existence. That kind of money could be game-changing for Kiva. But as we talked more, it was clear there was a catch. The man on the phone explained that his company was not interested in donating the money to Kiva's operational expenses, nor did it want to divide up the $10 million into $25, $50, or $100 gift certificates for the firm's employees and clients to use to make loans on the site. That would take too much time, he said. His company simply wanted to dump the money into the system we'd built somehow, have it divvied up to needy entrepreneurs throughout the world, and then get it back. I asked, in a dozen different ways, if he was open to any other solution—especially one that would engage the thousands of staff and clients his company represented—but he wasn't interested. He didn't have the time to deal with something like that.

While the entrepreneurs on our site would have obviously put that kind of funding to good use, it would have come without any actual lenders on the other side of the exchange. There would be no connective experience between lender and borrower—an integral part of our mission. Lenders would not get to browse profiles of borrowers on the site, choose a person whose story resonated, lend, get updates and repayments, and so on. Plus, because we were still relatively small and only had so many MFIs to post borrowers on the site, in the many months it would have taken for Kiva to direct that faceless $10 million to one entrepreneur at a time, a long line of potential lenders eager to get involved would have had to wait their turn. Though Kiva was still new, we were growing faster every day—almost too fast. We had more lenders wanting to get involved than we knew what to do with, and we were continually running out of loans on the site. Our biggest struggle at the time was keeping up with that demand by quickly but responsibly finding MFIs to post more entrepreneurs on the site.

So I swallowed hard and told him, "No, thank you." I then pointed him to some other great organizations that I thought would be a better fit for his money. He was flabbergasted. How could I possibly turn down $10 million? Was I crazy? I again walked through the options that would be a fit for Kiva. He wasn't interested. So I told him with confidence, "We really are grateful that you thought of us. But Kiva is about connecting people—and your contribution, as you've described it, wouldn't help us do that. So as generous as the offer is, it's not a fit for us."

I'll be honest, turning down such an enormous amount of money felt a little crazy. Had the company been a bit more flexible, it could have been a huge opportunity for us. But as it was, the opportunity was one we knew we could not accept. Taking that $10 million and simply dumping it into the system would have led us to drift from our core mission. In fact, the potential cost of taking that money would have been to turn away up to four hundred thousand individual lenders (if they each loaned $25).

Saying no to opportunities that don't match your mission, no matter how tempting they are, is the same as saying a resounding yes to the goals you have already committed yourself to. This is precisely what Katherine meant when she proudly claimed, "I am the bananas!" She had decided that she would focus on selling bananas and that all else would be secondary to this mission; that meant saying no to selling anything else. Certainly there were years when I bet she was tempted to sell other crops. But instead she chose to stick to her mission. And by doing so, she not only thrived, she built an identity for herself that everyone around her recognized and accepted. In the end I believe she was better off because of her focus and clear sense of direction.

Your mission is your identity and your guide. It tells the world, and serves to remind you, exactly who you are and who you are not. An organization that can craft a strong mission statement, share it with the world, internalize it as a team, and make tough decisions based on it has the chance to make a truly unique impact.

Raj the Rickshaw Driver

TAKE THE SIDE STREETS

Jaipur, India
2013

I clutched my map of Jaipur with one hand and the seat of the rickshaw with the other. I asked the driver, Raj, for the tenth time, "Are you sure this is the best route?" He turned to look back at me, flashed a quick smile, and wobbled his head a little, an Indian version of a nod in the affirmative. "It is," he said, for the tenth time. I smiled and thanked him as I subtly checked my map for any kind of validation I could find.

After less than a week in Jaipur I still didn't have a good lay of the land, and had absolutely no idea where we were. So I closed my map, sat back in the seat, and sighed. My only option was to trust Raj and enjoy the ride.

At first, this was easy. Raj seemed trustworthy. In fact I had chosen him from a lineup of other transportation options— dozens of other bicycle rickshaws, motorbikes, regular taxi-cabs, shuttles, and even a big bus that happened to stop right in front of me just as I was deciding which mode of transportation to take—because Raj had been the least pushy. A handful of acquaintances who had been standing next to me, all of whom had also attended the Jaipur Literature Festival earlier that day, had climbed into a large van to head back to our hotel. There wasn't room for all of us, so I waved them on and hopped aboard with Raj. He was the only rickshaw driver who wasn't barking at me like the others, insisting their bikes were the best, or that they would give me a special rate. He seemed patient and respectful and therefore, I concluded, a person of integrity.

Sure enough, for the first few minutes, the ride was exhilarating. We started our journey right before the sun began to set. Jaipur, known as the Pink City, earned its name as the sunset bloomed around us, warming up the sky and streets and buildings. Then the fiery sunset burned out to give way to an ashen dusk. Lights flickered on and nightlife began to come alive around us as we whizzed by small shops, street vendors, and noisy restaurants. Everything sparkled and hummed. It was lovely to witness in the open air.

As our ride continued and night fell, the atmosphere became heavy and thick with pollution. We puttered along in the throng of traffic, constantly weaving in and out among other bicycle taxis and myriad other vehicles, not to mention pedestrians, who were packed along the road. I was sure we were hitting every bump and pothole on the pockmarked street, and my rear end began to ache from sitting on the hard metal seat. I held on so tightly as we swerved and lurched that my hands felt tingly and numb.

Our pace slowed, then stopped. I was gulping exhaust and starting to get a headache. I began to regret hiring this rickshaw. Why hadn't I just taken a regular taxi or waited for the hotel shuttle to return?

I asked Raj what he thought was causing the pileup. Why were we stopped? Had there been an accident? Raj chuckled. "You are in India," he told me. This was normal. It was just what happened, especially in the evenings, he told me. I felt impatient. I had to get back to the hotel and get ready for a dinner that started in an hour, a big event in a completely different area of the city. I expressed my worry and asked Raj what he thought I should do. More than once I had found myself in situations like this—stuck in a taxi, at a halt in some big city's traffic—and found that the best solution was often to get out and walk or to find a subway or other public transportation. I asked if there was a bus I should catch instead, or maybe a car could make its way across town faster? He laughed. "No, no, this is best. I will get you there."

I leaned back into the hard seat, took a deep breath, and decided to see if he was right, at least for a few more minutes. I willed myself to be patient, and decided I may as well get to know Raj a bit better, since we were going to be awhile. I asked him about his life. Was he born in Jaipur? Did he have children? How long had he been driving this rickshaw? Did he enjoy this work?

He shared readily and with great animation. He told me about his four young children. He expressed gratitude for the chance to work and support them. He said he especially enjoyed meeting people from other places, which is why he tried to pick up customers from hotels, restaurants, or other spots that might attract visitors. He was delighted to know I lived in Los Angeles; he mentioned half a dozen other customers he'd met from various places in California but told me that he had never met someone from L.A. I felt like I was helping him complete a collection of sorts.

Raj did seem to be content in his work. Despite the dilapidated condition of the rickshaw—every part rusted, dented, bent, squeaking, wobbly, or in some other way falling apart—he handled the vehicle with grace and precision. Going around turns, he'd gently pump the brakes in such a way as to avoid the loud squeaking noise they seemed to want to make so badly. When he stood and put all his weight on the pedals to accelerate, he barely held on to the handlebars, which seemed not to be bolted on securely.

Talking to Raj had distracted me, and I realized suddenly that we had started moving again. Slowly but surely, Raj was weaving around cars and buses stopped on the highway. I noticed that we were moving even though most others weren't. And then, as soon as he was able, he turned off the main road onto a smaller thoroughfare. This road had lighter traffic, and he was able to move even more quickly, zigzagging around the other larger vehicles with more ease.

After another few minutes, Raj turned onto another smaller street with even fewer cars. We wound our way through less busy and less well lit streets of Jaipur. Where was this guy taking me? We were definitely off the beaten path, in pockets of the city that were totally unfamiliar to me. Despite the friendly conversation we had been having, suddenly I felt uncomfortable and suspicious. As the street became less and less populated, I grew more nervous. And when we turned onto an alley with no streetlights and almost no other vehicles at all, that nervousness became genuine alarm.

Most rickshaws in India are built in such a way that the driver sits in front of the passengers. Raj's vehicle was like this, so unless he turned around to talk to me or was looking in the rearview mirror, I could study my map in relative privacy, without risk of offending him. I did so, intently, until I'd catch him glancing back at me, smiling. I tried not to look alarmed.

I asked, "Are we close? Shouldn't we have arrived by now? Is this really the best way?" Raj just smiled again and responded, "Yes. Best way."

I sized him up. Raj was a short, thin man, wearing a threadbare shirt and trousers that were much too big for him, and sandals too large for his feet. I definitely outweighed him. Just in case he turned out to have intentions to kidnap me after all and I had to fight him, I surmised, I could take him. Or, I considered, maybe I would be better off outrunning him. Then again, he was a local and I had no idea where I was. My imagination ran wild with scenarios of confrontation and escape.

We had been riding for quite a long time now. I still didn't want to offend Raj, but panic had set in. "Raj, I would like to go back to the main road, please." He didn't hear me. Or he pretended not to. I was too scared to repeat myself and verify which was true.

In just a few more minutes we made our way back to the main road. Instead of turning onto the main street and packing ourselves into the throng, we cut directly across the intersection, winding through the standstill traffic. And then, to my utter amazement, there we were in front of my hotel.

Raj pulled to a stop and then hopped out of his seat with more energy than I thought was possible for a man who had been pedaling for that long. He smiled and gestured to my map, which I had clearly not hidden well enough from him along the ride. I handed it over and with his finger he traced the route we had taken. "Best way," he said once more. The path had been circuitous, but as he had proven, it had been the fastest.

My acquaintances on the shuttle? I saw them later on that night at the dinner—they showed up almost at the end of the event— and learned that they had arrived back at the hotel nearly an hour after I had.

In following his own path, Raj had beaten everyone else. He reminded me that sometimes ignoring the crowd and finding your own way is the best strategy to get to your destination.

CHAPTER 7

Walk Your Own Path

Break Up with the QB

In the late spring of 2005, just after Kiva's pilot round of loans had been distributed and a few months before we were set to officially launch, Matt and I were approached by two entrepreneurs who were also trying to develop their own venture in the microfinance space. Early into our initial conversation with them, they proposed that we join forces.

One of the founders had been an integral force behind one of the most successful web start-ups at the time. He struck us as smart and savvy, and through his previous work he had gained access to Silicon Valley's most elite circles. The other founder was also well-connected and had deep experience in the nonprofit world. She was a charismatic figure, and presented herself as someone whose involvement (or lack thereof) had the power to make or break an idea's ability to succeed.

We were flattered and somewhat confused by their invitation to partner with them; they seemed to have everything already going for them, and we had barely gotten started. But pairing up with this duo offered an intriguing opportunity, so we didn't ignore their offer. We asked them more questions about what they were doing, and how they thought we could work together. It was true, similarities did exist between our two ideas: We both wanted to innovate in the microfinance sector, we both wanted to give everyday people new options to empower entrepreneurs, and the timing of both ventures' beginnings did seem uncanny.

On the other hand, the similarities between the two organizations seemed superficial somehow. It wasn't clear that our core values aligned, and we definitely had different styles. For instance, we each used drastically different language to talk about our work; theirs seemed very business-focused and sophisticated to me, and ours felt simpler and more accessible. They spoke of users, we spoke of people. They talked about transactions, we talked about relationships. They referenced untapped markets and consumer trends, and we just talked about the kinds of markets where our entrepreneurs sold fish or vegetables or cooking oil. There were also vast differences in our visions. Kiva's was to become a portal for everyday people to lend directly to entrepreneurs; theirs was to create a securities marketplace for people to invest in microfinance institutions, as one would invest in the stock market.

Despite the obvious disparities between the two ventures, we remained intrigued by the possibility of working with such formidable people and continued to engage in conversations with them. As we did, and as we learned more and became even more intimidated by who they presented themselves to be, a sobering realization occurred to us. At this stage, after we had learned so much about them, rejecting their offer to partner would probably offend them and turn them against us. Choosing *not* to partner with them meant choosing to compete instead. At that stage, the idea of going head-to-head with a start-up like theirs was incredibly daunting and, we assumed, would inevitably mean losing. They had access to incredible resources and would inevitably tap their vast network of powerful individuals and companies to support their endeavor. These were not the kind of people you'd want to make your enemies.

We finally concluded, primarily out of fear, that we should give the partnership a go and try to work together. We decided that sacrificing a little control in the short term would give us greater access to resources we needed and lead to long-term gain. And yet even at the moment we said yes, I felt uneasy. But, I kept reminding myself, we would be crazy to turn down the opportunity.

Falling asleep one night, a few days after we had begun working with the other venture, I had a flashback to a time in high school when James McAllister, our high school's superstar football quarterback, asked me out on a date. James was the kind of suburban demigod that after-school TV specials are made of: He was tall, muscled, had sandy blond hair and misty blue-green eyes, and walked with a bit of a swagger. He was not the kind of guy who usually talked to me unless it was about homework. Don't get me wrong, he was perfectly nice, and I wasn't a pariah. We just came from different groups. People like James didn't really hang with people like me, let alone date people like me, or so I thought. His type seemed to be more tall, blond, cheerleader gorgeous than short, brown-haired, AP History chic. So when he asked me out one day between classes at the water fountain, as soon as I got over my initial shock and processed what was happening, I automatically said yes. It was a no-brainer. It seemed to be part of the script: Hot guy asks out girl, and she says yes, of course. No rational social animal would have said no to the offer. Go out with the QB, and you might as well start writing your homecoming queen acceptance speech. *Everyone* loved James. Therefore *I* loved James. Right?

Going out with James was fun, at first. Probably a little too much fun. He drove a bit too fast. He kept me out past curfew. He took me to my first party where there were no parents but plenty of alcohol (whereas I wouldn't touch a drink until my twenty-first birthday, and even then it was a toast of champagne with my grandma). Things with James were definitely exciting. But I knew I had to watch out for myself when I was with him. I didn't want to suddenly become that other, all-too-familiar character on those after-school TV specials: the nice girl who ended up making bad choices. It's not that James was a bad guy. It's just that, as I confirmed over time, he wasn't the guy for me, and to make it work I would have had to change important parts of who I was. Around James,

I felt pressure to become someone I was not. So after I had had my share of fun, I broke up with him in a movie theater, in the middle of a movie I hadn't wanted to see in the first place, and walked away.

The next day, my girlfriends at school thought I was crazy. How could I break up with James? *He was so cool! He was so handsome!* He was so . . . everything. I couldn't explain it very well to them, but I knew I had made the right choice.

Fast-forward back to the future: Being invited to work with those two hotshot Silicon Valley entrepreneurs was like getting asked out by the high school quarterback all over again. No rational, ambitious aspiring entrepreneur would say no to their offer to partner. Work with them, and the gatekeepers of Silicon Valley would welcome us into the fold. So, predictably, we ended up saying yes to those two ambitious, successful entrepreneurs.

Over the following few months we poured tremendous time and energy into pursuing a joint venture with them. We openly gave our new partners access to everything we had. We shared everything we had learned, every version of the business plan we'd drafted, all of the research we'd considered, every piece of data we had gathered on our entrepreneurs, and even the technology we'd built.

They were much more secretive with us, keeping their cards (and their code) close to their chests. And strangely, all the things we shared seemed to be ignored, or get swallowed up and absorbed into their vision. They didn't seem to understand our ideas. Or, more accurately, they understood everything but seemed to like their own ideas more. We began to doubt ourselves and our view of the world. Were they right? Were we wrong? They were, after all, older and more experienced, and they made very convincing arguments about why they should be the clear leaders. Soon we stopped trying to formulate counterarguments when they'd push back on our ideas and, in general, we weren't very aggressive about standing up for ourselves. We willingly gave ourselves over to their leadership. While they agreed to "let" us continue with Kiva's round of pilot loans, which we had begun a few weeks before meeting them, they insisted that from then on they would be the faces and voices of the new company that we would start together and that Matt and I would work behind the scenes. We gave over all control because, after all, we believed we wouldn't survive without their support.

Our acquiescence seemed only to make these other two entrepreneurs more power hungry. Within a few short weeks it became clear that they wanted to run the show completely and were doing their best not just to marginalize our involvement but to eliminate it. We were treated like pawns rather than partners. In one instance, they held a meeting with potential new team members without us, and my role and title were offered to someone else without my knowledge. On another occasion, they pitched potential investors and partners, again without us, and we later learned that our names had been removed from the pitch deck altogether. We even discovered they were working behind the scenes to convince various microfinance institutions to sign noncompete agreements against Kiva, so that these MFIs would be bound by contract never to work with us in the future.

Our so-called joint venture looked drastically different from what we'd originally envisioned for ourselves. And our dream of the recognition, the funding, and the contacts our powerful co-founders could provide was quickly losing its allure. Matt and I decided that we needed to take back control of everything that had originally been ours. Even if we had to go it alone, we wanted to get back to our authentic vision.

Though we knew this was the right choice, some of our closest friends and mentors at the time questioned our thinking. Were we sure it was the right call to walk away from such powerful people, and from such an influential, behemoth company? Their caution was understandable, but we knew in our hearts that breaking away was the only way to preserve our own identity and sanity.

We also knew we had to extract ourselves from the partnership very carefully. A sudden breakup might make our partners angry or, worse, trigger retaliation. They had everything they needed to steal the idea for Kiva and just do it themselves. This terrified us. We knew we needed to devise a strategy that would allow us to step away slowly and safely.

In late July 2005, after an all-night discussion, Matt and I agreed that the first step in our strategy would be, counterintuitively, feigned acqui-escence. We decided we would give up everything else that had been left on the table, and relinquish all control to them for a period of time. We thought this might neutralize them and win more of their favor, giving us a chance to part ways gracefully and eventually rebuild Kiva from scratch. So we spent a week or two giving ourselves over completely to their demands. We began agreeing to many of the humiliating ultima-tums that we had been fighting, including taking myself out of a prom-ised leadership role, agreeing that Matt and I did not need to be considered co-founders of the venture anymore (upon reflection, hav-ing four co-founders seemed like too many, they said), and consenting to several other ridiculous measures. Throughout the process, however, we made sure not to do anything that would harm our ability to be free of them as soon as possible. For example, we never signed any legal doc-uments that would have locked us into the partnership—a significant detail that gave us a great deal of protection.

After a week or two of acquiescing, while going along with their way of doing things, we also tried to make it painfully obvious to them that we, as a team, were not going to be a good fit in the long run. They did not respond well. Frustrated and offended, they got even more aggres-sive. They belittled us and threatened to marginalize our roles further (which seemed almost impossible to do at that point). I was reduced to tears.

It seemed obvious that, despite our attempt to comply with them and defuse things, parting ways gracefully wasn't going to happen. So we began to work on a Plan B strategy. We backed off, and again went into a period of acquiescing to their demands. But on nights and weekends outside of our work with them, we built up our original version of Kiva enough to stand on its own so we could formally part ways and relaunch it immediately once we left. We wanted to establish ourselves so we could begin again from a position of as much strength as possible. We figured, even if our parting was messy, we could pursue our original vi-sion for Kiva for a little while before they'd catch up and compete with us. We did this still thinking that, if and when they did try to copy what we were doing, they'd still eventually win. But we figured that a few months of pursuing our dream before we were beaten was better than never having made the attempt at all.

One night in late August 2005, the four of us had dinner, and we told them of our final decision to separate from them. We broke it off. They were angry, but this time they knew we were not going to be dissuaded.

As Matt and I walked away from that dinner, with every step we felt lighter. The next day we went back to pursuing the Kiva we had originally envisioned. We cut away the excess stuff that our former partners had wanted to add to our initial, simple product. Immediately, we felt better. We felt like ourselves again.

Just two months later, in October 2005, we issued a press release announcing our official launch. It was just *us*, and just our one simple idea. We could no longer boast any big alliances or famous supporters. There was no fanfare, and we no longer had the backing of a Silicon Valley giant. But still, much to our surprise, things soon took off. The rest is history.

In the end, Kiva remained independent and able to pursue its mission without compromise. The other two folks eventually launched their own organization in partnership with the Silicon Valley behemoth. While they existed as well for a few years, their product never really took off, and the venture shut down in 2014. Some folks say that their partnership with the larger tech company was a double-edged sword, providing support and resources but also hampering their ability to take risks and evolve quickly. Had we continued the partnership with them, I am sure now that Kiva never would have happened.

Crucially, Matt and I learned a powerful lesson about the importance of staying true to ourselves and our path, despite what everyone else around us seemed to think. If you believe in yourself and your idea, don't change to gain the endorsement of someone else, even if the whole world tells you that they are better, or stronger, or *right*, and that you are wrong. Stand alone if you have to. Don't be afraid. If your intentions are genuine, if your position is strong, and if your vision is clear, you will not be standing alone for long.

Get Away from the Group

Raj found a unique route for us to get home. He broke away from the traffic. He avoided the crowd. He didn't really care that everyone else was trying to make progress by going a different course. He wasn't afraid to be making his own way (with me along for the ride, of course).

Being on the outside of the group will give you a new vantage point. It will allow you to get a fresh perspective on a particular problem, and it might be just what you need to find a better, more innovative solution. This is why people who were never "on the inside" in the first place sometimes come up with breakthrough ideas that others have been trying to come up with for decades. Newcomers are often either unaware of or happily detached from the rules. They aren't wedded to precedent, so they can brainstorm without the same baggage or fear that an expert might have who has based his entire career on a particular way of thinking.

Entrepreneur, venture capitalist, author, and Kiva board member Reid Hoffman said at a 2011 speech at Berkeley: "Always think creatively and boldly. Where do you see a massive opportunity? Where do you think something is going to change, where you see something that most other people don't see? Part of being a successful entrepreneur is to be contrarian and to be right." Hoffman urges entrepreneurs to find these kinds of opportunities, to find ways to see things that other people don't see, and to challenge the status quo with a bold new way of looking at the world.

I had encountered these ideas before in an unexpected place: my sophomore philosophy of science course at Bucknell University. The first text assigned was Thomas Kuhn's *The Structure of Scientific Revolutions,* an analysis of the evolution of science and scientific thought. Kuhn explained how scientists don't work alone; they are instead part of scientific communities with sets of agreed-upon beliefs. Normal science operates within these sets of beliefs, or "paradigms," and many scientists' research, Kuhn claimed, is "a strenuous and devoted attempt to force nature into the conceptual boxes supplied by professional education."

But sometimes scientists observe things that do not fit existing paradigms (Kuhn called these "anomalies"), and when enough strong anomalies build up and validate each other, a new paradigm emerges and the old one crumbles. These shifts are scientific revolutions, "tradition-shattering complements to the tradition-bound activity of normal science." Scientific revolutions happen slowly, because by their nature they threaten the status quo. Remember Galileo, who was put under house arrest for claiming that the Earth revolved around the sun and not the other way around?

Kuhn's description of how paradigms shift and entire worldviews change is relevant far beyond scientific communities. We are all part of communities with agreed-upon, foundational beliefs. Deep down, conscious of it or not, we think we know something about what the world is like, and we gravitate toward others who think similarly. It's easy to go about our days without stopping to question our fundamental assumptions, though they can limit what we're capable of seeing and believing as possible. So usually, we're open to interpreting the world only in ways that perpetuate what we—and our communities—already believe to be true.

Thankfully, anomalies happen anyway. We get shaken up, surprised, or just baffled by life. We get hints that the world might be different from what we thought. This happens with greater frequency when we surround ourselves with the unfamiliar. Our lack of knowledge or experience suddenly becomes an asset when we are immersed in newness. It's easier to get surprised here. It's more likely we might have a fresh insight or a "crazy" idea, simply because we are seeing everything for the first time.

It's easy to shun these insights and to tell ourselves, "No, that can't be true," or "I must be crazy," or to listen to others' voices, which insist, "That's just not the way things are." But sometimes we're not crazy, and we've gotten a glimpse of something new and true, something that could actually redefine the status quo. Sometimes we really do glimpse a way of seeing things that no one else has before—or that no one else has been brave enough to speak up about yet.

To have more of these "aha" moments and get a fresh perspective, give yourself permission to take a different path once in a while. Get comfortable traveling in uncharted territory. Don't worry if everyone else thinks you're crazy. If you believe you have found a new and better way forward, blaze that trail. You just might be the first one to make a new path that the rest of us will one day follow too.

Clay the Confectioner

TREAT EVERYONE LIKE *OHANA*

Honolulu, Hawaii
2012

Over half a century ago, a boy named Clay would visit his neighborhood's candy shop, and every time without hesitation he would say, "I want to own this store one day!" Four decades later, in 1996, Clay's dream came true. He became the fourth proprietor of Doe Fang candy store, in the Aina Haina shopping center in Honolulu, Hawaii.

For fourteen years, seven days a week, Clay worked in that store. He put his heart into everything he did. He invented new concoctions, and sold his popular "Magic ICEEs" and other treats to many loyal fans. But all the while, he believed there was something deeper happening—something much more significant than simply selling candy. He believed the interactions that took place in his store could be "a way to love people, through serving every single guest, no matter their background, as *ohana*." (*Ohana* is the Hawaiian word for family.)

Still, business was tough. But Clay, who had by then become affectionately known to his customers as "Uncle Clay," persevered. He believed this was his mission in life, and so giving up was not an option for him. One by one, he sold his possessions to keep hold of Doe Fang. At one point, ten years in, he even decided to sell his last major personal asset—his house—in order to keep the shop open.

Then, in 2007, after sipping down a delicious Hawaiian Superman ICEE at Doe Fang, Uncle Clay's nephew, Bronson Chang, was struck with inspiration. Bronson envisioned a new future for Doe Fang. He believed he could help Doe Fang expand, opening new locations outside the Aina Haina shopping center and eventually far beyond Hawaii to reach thousands of new customers around the world. Bronson saw a future with "countless generations tied together in pure aloha tradition and experiences at the store, a place where Hawaii's beauty, magic, and aloha could be experienced all around the world." While most Americans know that *aloha* can be used as a greeting in Hawaii, it has much broader meaning as well. Technically, *aloha* in the Hawaiian language means affection, peace, compassion, and mercy. For Bronson, the term encompasses a culture and a way of life. It means living as a vessel to express a great, universal love to all human beings. Uncle Clay welcomed his nephew with open arms.

Bronson shared his vision with Uncle Clay, and told him that he wanted to join the family business upon graduation. The two began to plan. They wanted to continue offering Hawaii's iconic snack of "shave ice" but also wanted to give something more, providing guests a space to connect with one another, and eventually to give back to the community. Bronson, who was at the time a freshman at the University of Southern California, designed his studies around classes that he believed might help him best reenvision the store. Three years passed quickly and upon his graduation in 2010, Bronson was chosen as the class's baccalaureate speaker. The topic of his speech: his vision for his uncle's store. He shared his dream with his entire class, entitling his speech, "Pure Aloha." His heartfelt words were met with a standing ovation and many tears. A few weeks later he returned home to Hawaii and joined Uncle Clay as an equal partner in the venture, and together they relaunched the candy store as Uncle Clay's House of Pure Aloha (HOPA) in 2011.

I met Bronson right around this time, when I was teaching a social entrepreneurship course in the business school at USC. I had heard about Bronson from my students. Many of them had deep admiration for their charismatic, intelligent classmate. Everyone knew of Bronson as the "Pure Aloha entrepreneur" with a vision and plans for HOPA, and that Bronson would need investment capital to realize his vision. One of my students mentioned to Bronson that he might want to consider using ProFounder, the company that my friend Dana Mauriello and I were just launching to help entrepreneurs raise investment capital for their start-ups or small businesses from their friends, family, and community. I met Bronson to talk to him about whether or not ProFounder might be a fit, and over the following weeks, Bronson and Uncle Clay became ProFounder's first customers.

Using ProFounder's tools, Bronson and Uncle Clay created an online pitch that included a video explaining why they needed to raise money, financial projections, an investment term sheet, and more. They then used the site to invite friends, family, and longtime House of Pure Aloha customers to invest in their business in return for 2 percent of revenues over the next four years, as well as other bonuses such as private tastings of new shave ice flavors. They successfully raised $54,000 from nineteen people, including several classmates of Bronson's from USC. Since then, they have made notable improvements to the space, and in less than three years have served over one hundred thousand guests.

Looking back, in every way, the House of Pure Aloha fundraising campaign (or "raise") unfolded perfectly. Bronson and Uncle Clay were beloved in their community and had a track record of success. They extended highly personalized, thoughtful invitations to the people around them who believed in them and wanted to support them. They articulated their vision for expansion and their need for capital clearly. They chose an ambitious but achievable amount of money to raise, building an itemized budget from the bottom up and sharing their goals openly through the website. They created terms that would be sustainable for them and valuable to their investors, and took the time to explain the business, risks, and revenue projections in a way that was easy to understand. Bronson and Uncle Clay followed up politely but persistently with potential investors and made themselves available to answer questions personally. They hosted investor conference calls and in-store meet-ups, which helped people feel comfortable and meet fellow supporters. Watching them do all of these things, Dana and I were in awe. We expected our first customers to need a lot of help and hand-holding, but quite honestly, Bronson and Uncle Clay helped us. They taught us some powerful lessons about how to build, nurture, and gain support from a phenomenal community.

Very few of the investors in HOPA's raise on ProFounder were professional investors. Most were just friends, family, customers, and others who believed in Bronson and Uncle Clay's vision, shared their values, and wanted to see them succeed. Bronson and Uncle Clay believed their work had a purpose—spreading pure aloha— above and beyond crafting shave ice. This gave their work unique, larger-than-life meaning and drew people in, making them not only willing but grateful to invest in something that mattered to them, to their community, and even perhaps to the world. By taking the time and care to treat so many people around them like *ohana*, like family, they had built up the most important asset any small business could ask for: a large group of loyal, dedicated fans eager to help them grow. It was the strength of HOPA's extraordinary community that allowed Uncle Clay and Bronson to achieve the next step in their dream.

In 2012 I visited the House of Pure Aloha in person. My husband, Reza, my six-month-old twin boys, and I got to spend an afternoon with Bronson and Uncle Clay. There is truly something special about HOPA. The spirit of love and family is palpable. It permeates the place. One of my babies, Cyrus, slept in the stroller as the other one, Jaspar, held on to Bronson's hands and bounced on his knee, all the while staring wide-eyed at Uncle Clay, who was smiling a huge smile, clapping, and singing a Hawaiian song to him.

As we enjoyed the delicious shave ice and other treats in the store, I had the chance to ask Uncle Clay if his secret to success was as simple as it sounded. Without missing a beat he smiled and responded, "It's more than treating people nicely. It's understanding that you are connected to them for life, even if it is the first time they are walking in the door. At the House of Pure Aloha there are no strangers. There is only *ohana* yet to be met."

One by one, Uncle Clay over the years built one of the most loyal, enthusiastic communities I've ever seen. He didn't do it out of a desire to have influence or power. He didn't aim to build a big network because he thought it might be beneficial to him one day. He simply believes that every single person who comes to HOPA is a unique member of his family, and deserves to be treated as such.

Reza, the boys, and I may have walked in the door as virtual strangers. But instantly Uncle Clay made sure that we were, indeed, *ohana*.

CHAPTER 8

Find Your Family

The Founding Team

I have always appreciated the support my friends and family has given me, but that support was never more crucial to me than in the first few weeks and months after my twins were born in 2011. They were tiny and needy, I was exhausted, and we could not have survived without the selfless support of our community. My parents were there from day one of the boys' lives, doing anything and everything they could to care for all of us. My mom even took six weeks off work to live with us, so she could be available around the clock. Many others came to stay for days at a time, jumping right in to hold, feed, or change a baby (or two), or even to cook dinner for us so we could focus on the twins. They all showed up, ready to help, because they loved us, felt connected to us, and already felt invested in these new little lives.

At the beginning, start-ups are a bit like babies too, and I believe that it takes a dedicated family to care for them well. Young ventures are usually small and vulnerable and frequently need immediate attention or care of some kind—sometimes in the middle of the night. While some people do manage to go it alone, having a community of supporters dedicated to the venture's success can mean the difference between surviving and truly thriving.

The team that nurtured Kiva in its earliest days acted like family. They were not there for the money—in fact that would have been impossible, since there was none to be had. They weren't there for power or prestige, since we didn't have those things either. Those first team members showed up because they loved what they believed Kiva could become. They believed in the same possibility for the future that we did, and shared the same values. They invested in it before it was proven, before it could give much back to them. They wanted to be a part of something meaningful. They wanted to be a part of something bigger than themselves.

The very first person to join us was Chelsa Bocci, one of Matt's childhood friends. She had recently left the finance industry and returned from a trip around the world revitalized and inspired. She had heard about our project through family friends, and immediately wanted to get involved. She shared our values, shared the vision, and instead of focusing on the risks and uncertainty, she embraced the chance to help create something that might one day help a lot of people. She jumped on board right away and started building.

It was just a few weeks after our launch, and we knew our first priority was to figure out a way to get more borrowers on the site. We needed to grow a team of people who could find entrepreneurs for us, beyond just Moses in Uganda, to meet the demand we were seeing from lenders. Chelsa took the lead on this, finding more MFIs to partner with Kiva through random connections and Internet searches. She often adopted a night-shift schedule, staying up until the wee hours of the morning to be able to call potential partner MFIs during their working hours and catching up on sleep during the day. Her hard work earned Kiva our first partners, in Bulgaria, Nicaragua, Gaza, and Cambodia, to work with us within just three months of our launch blog post. It was an incredible accomplishment in and of itself, but especially so considering Kiva's complete lack of a track record.

The next two folks to join our team in early 2006 were Jeremy Frazao and Fiona Ramsey, a couple who had just returned from an eye-opening experience in tsunami-torn Thailand. They were introduced to us by Brian Lehnen, my former boss and mentor from Village Enterprise. For the second (and not the last) time, Brian's help would be game-changing for us. Jeremy, a gifted developer, immediately dove into working on the site with Matt. They quickly made major improvements, and the website shifted from being a rudimentary three pages to a dynamic marketplace. Fiona's electric personality made her a natural PR guru. In fact, Fiona ran customer service, accounting, *and* PR that first year.

A few months later, Premal Shah joined the team. Premal had been living a sort of parallel life to ours, dreaming about a similar idea while working at PayPal. He had actually tried to post profiles of MFI clients he had met in India on eBay to see if people would respond. (The loan applicants were removed almost immediately by eBay's compliance department, but we all admired the bold move.) He brought to Kiva not just a shared vision but a powerful set of skills and experiences, and a huge amount of enthusiasm for our project. He was also, amazingly, able to broker a partnership with PayPal to waive transaction fees on Kiva's site. In an unprecedented commitment, PayPal agreed to donate free payment processing to Kiva, and still does to this day, saving the organization millions of dollars every year. And that was just the beginning of Premal's contributions.

Soon thereafter Olana Khan joined us. Olana brought not just a huge passion for microfinance and civic engagement, but experience in the tech world and operational know-how that Kiva sorely needed. From finding our first office to getting office equipment donated from her former employer, Google, to eventually making sure we all had health insurance and good HR policies and countless other best practices, Olana transformed our group into a real organization.

Other amazing team members followed, like Ben Elberger and Michelle Kreger, who turned down several other opportunities simply to volunteer with us. Kiva was smart enough to hire them as soon as the organization had funds to do so—and was lucky enough to hold onto them for many years after.

Kiva survived its infancy because of the selfless dedication of Chelsa, Jeremy, Fiona, Premal, Olana, Ben, Michelle, and all of our earliest supporters—Kiva's nuclear family.

Feed the Roosters First

And very soon, that small original family grew. But how? How do young organizations bring in more and more supporters? How do they engage others in a meaningful way? How do they create loyalty and ownership and even a sense of family among a wider group of people who might live far apart from one another, dispersed all across the world?

I learned the secret one day when I was feeding my chickens. Or they were at least temporarily my chickens. I'll explain.

Almost always, upon visiting a family's home in a rural village in East Africa, this happens: They greet you warmly. Everyone stops what they are doing and comes over to say hello and to tell you that you are very welcome there. They will then bring out the very best of what they have to offer you. Usually there is a meal, even if it's not a typical mealtime. You feel humbled and never get used to the irrational generosity that is showered upon you every single visit. You eat. And you eat. And you eat. And then you are served more until you must insist that you cannot fit anything else into your stomach. Finally, as you are leaving, the family will give a gift, maybe handing you a live, flapping, clucking chicken (or rooster or turkey), even if it is the only one they own. There is no polite option other than to accept the bird as a gift and carry it with you into the car or onto the bus or bike or whatever mode of transportation you are using to go home. If you travel by car or bus, the chicken can sit in your lap or on the floor. If you travel by bike, you will probably be told there is no choice but to tie the chicken's feet and hang it upside down from one of the handlebars the whole way back home. This is just what's done.

When you get back to where you are staying you have several choices:

(1) Eat the chicken for dinner. (2) Stall. Let the chicken hang out for a while until you get up the guts to kill it, clean it, and eat it for dinner. (3) Regift the chicken to some other family you will soon be visiting so you can avoid options 1 and 2, and someone else can make those decisions.

Mostly, I chose option 3. However, be warned: Chickens are very good at finding their way home, so if you are going to give your chicken to another person as a gift, make sure that person lives in a different village, as far away as you can manage. I have made the embarrassing mistake more than once of giving a chicken I had been given to another host, only to have the chicken run away and end up back with the original owner who gave it to me in the first place. The original gift giver then assumes that you either lost your gift along the way, or are rejecting it and meant to give it back. Both are extremely uncomfortable scenarios. Don't let this happen to you.

Sometimes it has taken a while before I have been able to visit a new village far enough away to regift the birds, so for a little while they become my pets. I name them, feed them, and just watch them interact with one another.

Once, while I was staying in Uganda, I had accumulated a good halfdozen chickens plus a rooster. I was staying in one of the nicest places I'd ever stayed in East Africa, a guesthouse with a tiny courtyard. I put the chickens and rooster in the courtyard, and one afternoon I grabbed a chair and my journal and sat near them in the courtyard. As I thought and wrote, I looked up every once in a while to see what they were doing. I also brought a few handfuls of seeds so I could feed them. To me, watching and feeding the chickens was fun. To my Ugandan hosts, watching *me* out there seemed to serve as entertainment.

At first I knelt down and offered the grain in my hands to the chickens to see if they would come to me. They steered clear. So I stood up, tossed it to them at a distance, and waited. The rooster was the first to approach it. He clucked, looked around, picked up a bit of food with his beak, but then, instead of eating it right away, he dropped it back on the ground. He did this again and again. I wondered if the food was bad, or if the rooster was sick. I walked over to the seed to examine it, causing the birds to scatter. Nothing looked unusual, so I stepped away again and waited. Again, the rooster did his routine. But then, as the other birds watched him, they began to eat. When they did, the rooster ate too.

That night, over dinner (a dinner that did not include chicken, for the record), I asked my Ugandan friend Michael about what I had seen. He chuckled and explained to me that nothing was wrong. The rooster was doing his job. "The roosters are like the leaders," he said. With this, Michael, who had kept chickens all his life, launched into a detailed lecture about rooster behavior. He explained to me that the rooster's actions communicated to the chickens that it was time to eat; he was inviting them to join in. The chickens often needed a rooster to be their guide and point out the food, and the rooster was programmed to play this role. Michael went on to explain that roosters are also vigilant protectors of their flocks, guarding them against predators and defending them when they are attacked. I heard more stories than I had ever wanted to about times when Michael had witnessed roosters fighting a variety of other animals. It was enough to make me push my dinner plate aside.

Still, I was glad to have gotten a cursory rooster education from Michael. He had reminded me of this truth: The best way to ensure the well-being of your team is to find strong leaders to join your organization, and then let them lead. The chickens weren't going to eat right out of my hands, but they would follow the rooster.

It sounds easy, but when you are doing work you care about deeply, and when the thing you value most is having an impact in the world, it can be a challenge to let other leaders in. Doing so requires humility, an ability to delegate, and an ability to give up control. You must have a genuine desire to see positive change happen, even if it means you aren't the person enacting that change every time.

Kiva's values as an organization are centered on equality and partnership with everyone involved. The goal has been to give people the freedom, the information, and the tools they would need not just to contribute themselves but to become leaders for Kiva in their own communities. As a 501(c)(3) nonprofit organization, Kiva is a publicly owned entity, so it made sense that all "owners" should be able to help make the organization better and stronger. For instance, there are dozens of robust independent communities of lenders, created across various social networking platforms; many of these lender-driven groups have provided valuable feedback and new ideas to Kiva over the years. On Kiva, lending teams are independent groups made up of individual lenders who form without Kiva's supervision or direction and who compete with one another to see who can lend the most. Anyone can create a team, and then track the team's collective lending together. Tens of thousands of people have self-organized such groups. Interestingly, the top two lending teams have traditionally been "Atheists, Agnostics, Skeptics, Freethinkers, Secular Humanists, and the Non-Religious," and "Kiva Christians," though lending teams are formed around a variety of affiliations and interests, from school and alumni groups to local communities to businesses to event-based groups and more. As of December 2014, there were nearly thirty thousand teams on the site.

If you have a strong vision for what you want to accomplish in the world, it can be scary to give away control to others, especially other strong leaders. But when those others are eager to help, they can manifest your vision in invaluable, sometimes surprising ways. They may contribute new ideas or take actions that you might not have imagined, and exceed your expectations—and you will get more accomplished than would have ever been possible without them.

Most teams will have natural leaders who emerge, who express the values of the organization and set a tone and an example by their actions. Empower these natural leaders. Provide them not just with permission but with extra tools and resources to influence others. Give them access to information that will help them understand the big picture. Offer them the power to make decisions about funding and the resources to reward their teams for their contributions. Encourage them to learn and grow. Let them take risks and have real responsibility over outcomes, even though that means that they will sometimes make mistakes.

Great leaders embody the values of your organization and express those values to others through all they do. Empower them and your organization will thrive. Make it easy for anyone who wants to get involved in what you are doing to find real, meaningful ways to participate. Give your leaders real control and real responsibility. They will attract others who share those values—building your community based on what matters to you.

CiCi the Tour Guide

FIND THE BOAT

San Diego, California
2011

Like Bronson and Uncle Clay, CiCi Sayer was one of Pro-Founder's earliest customers. CiCi owned a whale-watching and ecotourism business called Offshore Blue Adventures in San Diego, conducting a variety of whale- and dolphin-watching tours off the Southern California coast on a twenty-one-foot rigid inflatable boat (RIB). Her boat accommodated only six passengers, which kept the tours intimate, and was fast, quiet, and extremely stable in all but the stormiest conditions. A few years into her business, CiCi needed a new RIB, and decided to crowdfund the capital for this and several other items she needed to rejuvenate the business. Using ProFounder she made a detailed budget, listing each item she needed alongside its cost, so that anyone looking to invest could understand how the money would be used. Her total budget was over $90,000—with $65,000 of that designated for a new boat.

She spread the word about her fundraising campaign, but investors were slow to pitch in, and the contributions she did receive were small. It seemed that her $90,000 was much too far out of reach. CiCi began to get discouraged and considered giving up.

"I was ready to put my dream on the shelf and move to Lake Havasu to work as a ferryboat captain," she told me. "I had decided I would go work there for five years to save enough money to buy the boat I wanted."

After a few weeks of trying to raise the $90,000 but falling short, with her deadline fast approaching, she went to sleep one night resigned to the likelihood that she had failed. This meant she would have to give back the small amount of money she had already raised from investors. She fell asleep with a heavy heart.

Then, at 5:30 A.M., the phone rang. It was a friend of CiCi's who couldn't afford to invest a lot of money in her business but had been cheering her on the whole time. He had interesting news to share with her. He knew CiCi needed a new boat, and because he had read her fund-raising pitch carefully weeks earlier, he remembered exactly what kind she was looking for. This had been fresh in his mind when he saw an ad on the bulletin board of his local laundromat advertising a twenty-one-foot RIB—just what she needed—in "like new" condition, for only $18,000.

CiCi acted quickly. She adjusted her budget accordingly to reflect the new, significantly lower price of the boat, and suddenly she had just enough investment commitments to move forward with her plans! That very same day, CiCi purchased the boat, a new engine, and a trailer.

Because CiCi let other people in on her dreams, they helped her get what she needed in completely unexpected ways. While not all of them could contribute financially, what they could offer ended up being more than enough.

CHAPTER 9

Receive the Unexpected

Advice Over Money

I first met Bob King and his wife, Dottie, when I led a Village Enterprise donor trip in Kenya in 2005. We were there—along with a half-dozen others—to see Village Enterprise's work on the ground. Many of the individuals on the seven-day journey had donated significant amounts of money to the organization, and they were eager to meet some of the recipients and see some of the results that their generous donations had enabled.

It was just after 5 A.M. when Bob and Dottie burst in through the front door of the guesthouse where the rest of our group was sleeping, in that kind of heavy, post–jet lag slumber from which it's especially disorienting to be awakened. Even after strenuous overnight travel, Bob and Dottie were as loud and excited and fresh and wide-eyed as the rest of us were exhausted. After that entrance, I knew I was in for a very special experience over the next few days with these two. Bob and Dottie, septuagenarians at the time, were (and are) some of the most passionate, enthusiastic, resilient globetrotters I've ever met. They jumped right into the program, asked a lot of questions, took photos, had lots of direct conversations with the entrepreneurs we met during our trip, and overall became among the most active contributors to the group.

A few days into our trip, Bob and I sat in a van together, bouncing along through crazy Nairobi traffic en route to see some microfinance projects. I told him about Kiva, which was just about to launch our pilot round of loans, and I asked him how he thought I should go about bringing the best and brightest people into our community, about marketing strategies, and a million other questions. Most memorably, we also talked about fund-raising. I admitted that in the past I had felt uncomfortable at times when approaching people to donate to other nonprofits I had worked with, and Bob shared some wisdom from his own experience of being constantly approached for funds. (At the time, I had little understanding of the depth of Bob and Dottie's wealth or their incredible generosity. I later learned that the couple is known throughout Silicon Valley for their giving; in 2011 alone they committed $150 million to create the Stanford Institute on Innovation in Developing Economies, housed at the Graduate School of Business, one of the largest donations the university had ever received.)

Bob told me that the people who approached him for funding were usually well prepared, able to talk at length about their organization or about the campaign for which they were raising funds. But most of the time, these people seemed to have no genuine interest in hearing what Bob, who had built his wealth over a long and incredibly successful career in investing, might have to say about their project or plans. It was rare, he said, that anyone opened up a conversation by asking him to share something about himself, or by asking him what he thought about the nonprofit's work. They usually just went straight for his checkbook. They clearly saw him as a means to an end. This made me think of a silly cartoon image that I'd seen throughout my childhood. Remember the Tasmanian Devil, Taz, from *Looney Tunes*? That little brown marsupial with a ferocious appetite and a short temper who got so crazed and frantic that he'd spin around in a tornado of dust? When he was hungry, he'd look at Bugs Bunny as one big piece of food, like a big chicken leg or a steak. Certain fund-raising professionals seemed to view potential donors similarly; only instead of seeing a chicken leg, they'd see dollar signs.

For Bob, having his expertise overlooked felt disappointing and hurt-ful. I did not *ever* want to become a fund-raising Taz, and cause another person to feel like Bob felt sometimes. I asked him what his advice was for me. What could I do in my own fund-raising efforts to make sure I didn't inadvertently make others feel this way, while at the same time making it known that organizations needed money to pay staff and keep the lights on? He looked at me and said, "Don't treat people as a means to an end. If you just ask for money and ignore the person, you'll end the conversation quickly. Or, best case, they'll give you an earful of advice. But ask for their thoughts first, and get people involved, and if they are able to, they'll give. Ask for money, get advice. But start by asking for advice, and really trying to involve that person, and you'll get so much more, often including their financial backing. And then you'll have the best of everything."

I have never forgotten Bob's advice. In countless conversations with friends, volunteers, staff, donors, VCs, and anyone else who is involved (or who is considering getting involved) in something I care about, I remember that I am speaking to a person, not a bank account.

Understand and identify the unique contributions others can make. You do need people who provide financial support as a part of your community. But don't ignore the other things each individual can offer. Get people involved. Money is rarely the most valuable thing you can receive from another person who cares about your work and wants to help.

Asking for More

After Kiva formally launched, almost a year passed when we were unable to pay our earliest staff. We decided it was time to fund-raise for donations—not loans—to cover operational expenses and start paying salaries. At first we attempted to raise funds online from lenders, but this did not work out so well. After a very brief early experiment giving lend-ers the option to donate as well as to lend on the site, it became clear that people were getting confused. Because lending online was such a new idea, even mentioning the word "donation" or asking people to "give" instead of lend muddied the waters, and led to misunderstandings about our core product of a 0 percent loan. We had to double back, putting all of our efforts into emphasizing that Kiva was about lending—not donating—and removed the option to donate on the site altogether to avoid any confusion.

So we relied on raising funds off-line, in conversations with family, close friends, and our handful of board members. We received very few but very generous donations, a few of $10,000 or more at a time, and by the end of our first year we had raised about $125,000 in donations. But that money went quickly, and there were only so many people we knew who could write checks of that size. By the time our October 2006 board meeting took place we had only $15,000 in the bank. This was just enough for one more month of paid operations. While we had facilitated $500,000 in loans, we were close to running out of money to keep the lights on. We didn't know what we were going to do.

One board member had told us to call him if we absolutely ran out of options so he could liquidate some of his assets if needed, but we did not want to resort to that. As a last-ditch effort, we reluctantly decided we should reinstate the option for lenders to donate online alongside their loan, suggesting they contribute 10 percent of their loan value on top of the actual loan, so that a $25 loan to an entrepreneur would come with a $2.50 donation toward Kiva's operating expenses. We were quite worried that people would get upset, frustrated, or just confused again. After all, we'd been shouting from the rooftops that Kiva was a lending platform, and had been doing our best to get people to participate as lenders. We thought asking them for a donation as well might again steer people off course, or worse, seem demanding and backfire. But it seemed like the only option we had. So, we carefully rewrote the language around the request. We put up a picture of our office in the Mission District of San Francisco, with its crumbling brick and bars on the windows, and asked folks to help us pay the rent. And then we made it live on the site and hoped for the best.

Amazingly, asking for a tiny donation alongside a loan worked much better this time than it had just a few months before. It didn't cause much confusion and most lenders responded positively—they were happy to give as well as lend. Apparently, our few months of focusing on loans had worked and most people had gained a solid understanding of the loan product. Plus, a more careful articulation of the optional donation made it less confusing to participate.

Even more incredible, this positive response from lenders created a sort of flywheel effect. Their participation helped us make a solid case to other, bigger would-be donors that we were on the road to becoming a more sustainable organization, which made them more likely to donate too.

Then, just two weeks after Kiva's one-year anniversary, PBS's *Frontline/World* aired a special about us on Halloween night in 2006. The surge in traffic from this coverage served as the much-needed catalyst we had been hoping for. Within days, daily lending volume on the site had jumped to ten times what it had been before. Our partners stepped up and provided more and more borrower profiles on the site to keep up with the demand as best they could. Each unique profile, now from a wide range of places all around the world, contributed to an increasingly rich, colorful, varied community of entrepreneurs on the site: a spinach farmer in Cambodia, a carpenter in Gaza, a beekeeper in Ghana, a tailor in Uganda, a hot dog stand owner in Nicaragua, and so many more.

Kiva was in the clear. But we almost didn't make it. Lenders came to our rescue. We were afraid to request even more from them, but they stepped up. They surprised us. They proved that they were happy to support Kiva in ways above and beyond what we had expected, and taught us that we should never be afraid to show our needs and ask for help.

Answering Well

I locked eyes with the Queen. The Queen of talk, that is: Oprah Winfrey herself. She and Matt had been chatting like old friends in front of the bright lights and studio audience. And now she turned to me. Two cameras silently swiveled in my direction. It was the summer of 2007, and in the year and a half since we had launched Kiva, this was by far the most intense, pressure-packed moment I could remember. I was well aware that every word, every facial expression in those next few seconds could have an enormous impact on how the world saw Kiva and whether or not any of the millions of people watching would decide to come to the site and see what we were about.

My heart was pounding so hard I could hear the blood rushing through my head: a loud *whoosh-whoosh* in my ears. I tried to focus. What had Oprah just asked me?

I was pretty sure her question had been something general and open like, "How has all of this been for you?" which was good because I could say anything, but also bad because, well, I could say anything. I wondered if I looked as nervous as I felt under the hot lights, my eyelids and cheeks caked with layers of TV makeup. I kept getting distracted by all the sparkle, and by Oprah's shoes (which were gorgeous), and by how it sounded when President Clinton, who also sat onstage, used my name in a sentence.

You can't very well ask Oprah to repeat herself in the middle of a show. So I took a breath. I smiled. I blinked. I stared. *Think, Jessica! Think!!*

When HARPO Studios had called the Kiva office inviting us to be on *The Oprah Winfrey Show* with only two weeks' notice, we thought it was a prank phone call. The person on the other end of the line assured us this was real, and she was serious. She knew all about Kiva, the organization's most recent statistics, our personal story, and that we were going to be featured in President Bill Clinton's new book, *Giving*, which was coming out in two weeks. Oprah would be interviewing President Clinton about his book on the show, and we were invited to be on as a part of that episode.

We accepted the invitation and then scrambled to prepare. We practiced answering every possible question we could think of. We got haircuts. We went shopping for new clothes. We rented DVDs of old Oprah shows and watched them at night on our laptops. We even spent a precious few hundred dollars on a few hours with a very fancy PR person to get basic media training. To be honest, the training was not very helpful, but at least we could check it off the list.

And then, suddenly, the morning of the show arrived and we were backstage getting ready to go on camera.

I sat in a makeup chair in the green room as one person airbrushed my face with makeup while another flat-ironed the waves out of my hair, then carefully recurled it, brushed it, and teased it, so it ended up wavy again (looking to me exactly the same as before). Another person steamed my shirt. Another one picked lint off that shirt. Another offered me coffee so many times that I ended up with three cups scattered throughout the room, and I didn't even drink coffee. Just when I thought we were finished, another woman entered the green room holding a clipboard, looking more serious than the others. She approached us and, after a few niceties, got down to business. "Okay, guys. You're on soon and we need to go over your segment of the show. While nothing here is scripted, of course, I'd like to go over some possible questions Ms. Winfrey may ask you. And, based on our research of you, we've drafted some answers you might give in response to these questions."

I was floored. This was what they called "unscripted"? No one was going to tell me what to say! I'd say whatever I pleased, thank you very much.

Before I could protest, the woman began to read the possible questions Ms. Winfrey might ask, and suggested answers I might give based on quotes I had given before in other talks or interviews. The process totally disarmed me. As I listened to her rattle off possible answers, I calmed down. This stuff was *good*. Their team had done an incredible job patching together things I had said before, drafting answers that I would genuinely want to say. They were better than my own talking points.

That moment taught me a very important lesson about the art of answering—not just asking—a question. While at first I was downright offended by the idea that someone else thought they knew better than I did what I should say, when I just stopped and listened to their ideas, it helped me understand how they saw me and what they found interesting about our journey thus far.

Of course, once the show started and we were live, Ms. Winfrey asked me none of the questions we had reviewed backstage. Nothing even close. Her questions were open-ended and off the cuff. *Unscripted.* She'd asked me how the whole experience had been for me, and what I'd found most rewarding. My mind went blank for an instant. Then looking back at her, feigning confidence, I answered. I opened my mouth and began, "This has been a dream coming true every day for us. . . ." Then the words flowed. I described how amazing it had been to watch so many people lift themselves out of poverty. I spoke in mostly complete sentences. I used appropriate hand gestures. I got teary-eyed and cried just a little, but not so much that it got ugly. (This was not, by the way, the carefully controlled emotional response I learned in media training. I just tend to cry a lot.) And then it was over.

When the episode aired a few days later, I was in Swaziland on a work assignment for Kiva. I attempted to listen to a few minutes of the show over the phone with my mom while she held up the receiver to the TV speaker in her living room in Pittsburgh. As I kept in touch with the team over the next few days I learned that the show had caused such a spike in traffic to the website that the site had crashed—something we had anticipated. Over the next few days, hundreds of sympathetic souls donated over $100,000 to us so that we could buy bigger servers to handle the load next time Ms. Winfrey called.

Shona the Sculptor

LEARN AS YOU BUILD

Cape Town, South Africa
2012

Shona McDonald beamed with happiness as she watched one of her customers, ten-year-old Mary, roll off in the brand new wheelchair that Shona had made just for her. Mary was being pushed along by her parents and was flanked by her proud siblings, each one reaching out to keep a handhold on their young sister's shiny new chair.

People came from all over South Africa and beyond to see Shona.

Just a few days earlier, an older woman and her severely disabled five-year-old grandson had shown up seeking Shona's help. The child could not walk, so he was tied to his grandmother's back with a shirt and a folded-up bedsheet. Shona told me that this heartbreaking scene was not uncommon. "These mums just tie their bigger kids onto their backs like they did for their babies. Some carry them like this until they are teenagers and then everyone is in very poor condition. The mums can hardly walk at that point."

I was lucky enough to meet Shona, the visionary founder

and managing director of the South African company Shonaquip, in the spring of 2009 while writing case studies for Professor Garth Saloner (now dean at the Stanford Graduate School of Business). The case studies were developed in a partnership with Goldman Sachs's 10,000 Women initiative, and were intended to highlight talented women entrepreneurs around the world. As we sat in the shaded backyard garden behind her home in Cape Town, Shona told me her remarkable story.

In 1981, Shona's second daughter, Shelly, was born with several physical disabilities. Shelly was unable to speak, almost totally deaf, and was soon diagnosed with cerebral palsy. Shona and her family knew they would have to make some changes at home in order to properly care for Shelly. What they had not anticipated was how discouraging those around her seemed to be about Shelly's future: "I was shocked," Shona said. "Doctors were telling us how kids with these disabilities were useless. The specialist actually told me to just put Shelly in a home and have another baby—to start over, as if she didn't count for anything. It was incredibly sad and disempowering."

Shona immediately began to make adjustments in her day-to-day routine to care for Shelly. As realistic as she was about her daughter's needs, she also believed in Shelly's potential far beyond what the doctors had told her was possible. This belief was galvanized as, over and over again, Shelly responded to Shona's efforts to engage her and teach her new things. Shona sought out whatever tools and learning methods she could find, and using facilitated play, sign language, and symbols, she began to educate Shelly at home.

Shona constantly tweaked these tools and teaching materials to fit Shelly's needs. She adjusted basic household objects and furniture around Shelly to better suit her daughter's abilities, discovering that, for example, Shelly's position sitting in a chair or while lying down could have a strong positive or negative effect on her ability to engage in activities and control her movements. "I started to realize that if you couldn't sit properly and look at something or at the person teaching you, then communication just wasn't going to happen," she said. "If the child couldn't physically hold her body in the right position, it became impossible to teach them." Shelly's disabilities were so severe that just changing the height of her seat by adding a cushion or pillow beneath her was inadequate; she needed something much more fitted, something that could give her firm support at many different places on her body.

So Shona searched for better options for her daughter's needs. She could not find them. The majority of assistive devices for people with severe disabilities like Shelly's were uniformly standardized. As such, they were often useless for the people who needed them most: those who had the most complex disabilities. This was especially true for children. To Shona, it was crazy to think that a standard prop or device would work for most people. As she put it, it was like "buying false teeth over the counter at the supermarket or just having one strength of eyeglasses available for anyone with a vision impairment."

Drawing on her background as an artist and sculptor, Shona began to make her own equipment. At first, what she built didn't always fit right or was too awkward for Shelly to use. But Shona believed that the process of building equipment that worked would be similar to the way she sculpted. She knew a sculpture doesn't look like a sculpture at the beginning: the real art lives many layers inside the block of clay, wood, or rock. It has to be found over time within the object. She had to carve, sand, or chip away at the thing to discover the final shape. Only after a long process could the masterpiece emerge from the material. It was necessary to move through many versions of imperfection before finding the truly beautiful thing.

So she kept at it and made adjustments with her designs for Shelly. Little by little Shona was able to craft supports and

equipment that fit Shelly well, enabling her to sit up, communicate, learn, and thrive.

As Shelly grew and her needs constantly changed, Shona kept
up, creating new versions at each stage. Shona grew more
passionate in her beliefs that the right equipment meant a better
life for Shelly, and for others like her. She became convinced that a
properly designed chair, matched to the need of the person sitting
in it, was the key to ongoing growth and development. "You don't
just look at a chair and fit the kid into it the best way you can, you
need to look at the kid and then create the best chair for their
needs. Not the other way around."

Shona was so driven to pursue perfection with these devices that
by the time Shelly was two and a half years old, she had already
created a number of chairs, including a motorized wheelchair that
she designed and built in conjunction with some friends at the
University of Cape Town. This was the first motorized buggy ever
built in South Africa.

Shona soon began to create chairs and buggies for her friends'
kids with disabilities too. Demand was so high that she soon
worked on building chairs every day. She worked for free, but after
a while her friends insisted that she begin to charge for her work.
Shona reluctantly agreed, and officially registered Shonaquip as a
real organization in 1992.

Shonaquip has since grown significantly from a staff of two
operating out of Shona's garage to dozens of technicians, seamstresses, and therapists. The company now designs, manufactures,
and supplies mobility equipment, as well as augmentative and
alternative communication devices for people with moderate or
severe physical disabilities. To date, Shonaquip has directly assisted
over 70,000 children, and beyond this is admired for raising
awareness and changing perceptions of people with disabilities in
the communities it serves.

But I admire it most for its origins. Inspired by a great love for her daughter, and committed to giving her the best she could give, Shona began by building the best solution she could for a single person. With great love and care, she paid close attention to every detail and made small improvements, day after day. Over time, this led to the design of products that were markedly different from anything else available. She was a master of the iterative design process, and this process led to the creation of truly innovative products and a powerful organization that have served tens of thousands of children throughout South Africa and beyond.

CHAPTER 10

Invent. Iterate. Repeat.

Designing for Change

In the spring of 2007, Kiva was just a year and a half old and I was in the thick of my second year of business school at Stanford. I was eager for the start of a particular new course, called "Design for Extreme Affordability," offered in conjunction with the neighboring Design School (also known as the d.school) at Stanford. The course, fondly called "Extreme" among alums of the d.school, takes place across two quarters, and is a multidisciplinary project-based experience that teaches students to design products and services for the world's poorest people. Students work directly with outside organizations to solve real-world problems, culminating with the actual implementation of a project. I could not have dreamed up a more perfect way to learn about design thinking and design principles—and I was eager to learn from Jim Patell, who teaches the course, leads the d.school, and whom I had gotten to know throughout my previous years working at Stanford.

The class was divided into several diverse teams, each made up of business school students, engineering students, and liberal arts students. We were all assigned the task of creating innovative, radically low-cost, socially impactful products for farmers living in rural Myanmar. At first, my team decided to work on redesigning water pumps. We immediately came up with lots of ideas, but almost as quickly those ideas were shot down—for good reason. "We can't ask the women to use pedals like this," said one of my teammates, pointing at a sketch of what looked like a crude StairMaster exercise machine made out of metal and bamboo. "They will think the motion is too provocative. When they step up and down, and go back and forth like that, their hips wiggle. You know, like this." He did a little demonstration, and we all laughed. Half of our classmates had spent their spring breaks in the field interviewing and observing the kinds of farmers in Myanmar we aimed to serve, so despite our giggling, we took this information to heart.

Eventually, we chose instead to work on the issue of cheap water storage. This was a significant problem in Myanmar without an affordable solution. Often, farmers must pump water from a well, temporarily store the water as it is being pumped from underground, and then use cans to take the water across their fields to water their crops. People often dug simple holes in the ground to store the water for the short time between pumping and watering crops because it was a straightforward and low-cost solution. Yet a lot of the hard work from pumping the water up from the ground was lost, as a great deal of water was reabsorbed into the earth. Some wealthier families use concrete or metal containers to store the water after it has been pumped, and leakage issues were rarely a problem for them, but these solutions were much too expensive for most rural farmers. And a solution that was too expensive was not a solution. Affordability was our primary design constraint, and all else fell below this priority. For example, durability, a quality I had assumed was universally sacred, was low on the list for this assignment. Paying $50 for a product, even if it lasted a decade, was simply not going to be an option for the customers we were designing for. Instead, paying $5 for a solution, even if it only lasted for a few months and then would have to be replaced, would serve more people better. Something that was "built to last" but was pricey would sit on shelves forever next to items that were intentionally "built not to last" but were affordable.

Our team began to brainstorm about better ways to store water. We researched other water-storage options all over the world, but we also branched out and thought more broadly about how water was stored in other situations, for other uses. One day, we browsed a toy store for ideas. What could we learn from water balloons, fish tanks, and squirt guns? Our inspiration came when we stumbled upon an inflatable kiddie-sized swimming pool. The pool was round, with sides that angled slightly inward—the sort of shape you'd get if you took a very large cone, point up, and cut off the top 90 percent of it. The pressure from the water in the pool helped hold the sides up; in fact the sides flopped inward if the pool wasn't filled properly. The entire pool was made of soft, flexible plastic. It was lightweight, pretty durable, and easy to transport. We purchased the kiddie pool and some waterproof tarps, and went back to the d.school to make our own prototypes based on this design.

We cut and sewed our first water-storage bags, shaped somewhat like the kiddie pool. The construction was difficult and slow. We had to use very strong and thick thread and large needles, which frequently snapped in half trying to push through the waxy fabric. My sewing machine stalled several times, so we had to finish stitching together the seams by hand. We tried using duct tape instead to put together a second round of bags. The duct tape worked, but it took a very long time to make sure all points were sealed properly. Still, we felt we had a strong enough prototype to test it overnight. We filled it with water and left for the evening. The next day, we saw that there had been some leakage in the spots where we hadn't pressed hard enough to seal the tape to the tarp material, but overall the second version had been an improvement. So we took what we had learned and made a third version of the bag, which was both sewn and sealed with tape twice over. This worked even better than the other two. Again we tested it overnight to see if the seals would hold. They did! This process of slow improvement continued for many days until we got the design perfected.

Throughout the process, we were able to improve upon our model quickly because every team member played his or her part, bringing a unique perspective to bear on the task at hand. As our team tried to solve structural problems with the bag, the engineering students made meaningful suggestions about adjusting the angle of the wall or creating counterpressure. Other team members, some of whom were liberal arts students, helped us to understand the culture of Myanmar and to be realistic about how farmers would behave in real life. If we assumed some fact or anticipated some behavior from them that was unrealistic, they corrected us. For instance, we realized we were assuming that only adults would access water from the bag, so we had made the walls of the storage bag high, but in actuality we needed to consider the children's heights as well. Then, of course, the business-school students, like myself, tried to ask the right questions about what materials would be available locally, their costs, how distribution of the water-storage bags would work best, how a product like this might be marketed, and so on.

We made continual adjustments, and by the end we had a respectable product that would cost an end user only a few dollars. We were proud to have created an alternative that was more effective than just leaving water in a hole in the ground, and much more affordable than a heavy, hard plastic or metal holding container.

Our product was adopted by a d.school nonprofit partner and manufactured in Myanmar, and has been used by thousands of farmers. Even better, future student teams taking the "Entrepreneurial Design for Extreme Affordability" course continued to expand upon our idea, and improved our original water-storage bag in significant ways. A few years after we designed the first bag, another d.school team picked up where we had left off and experimented with different shapes, sizes, and materials for the bag, and came up with a brilliant construction process inspired by origami. This team realized they could use tarp material in the same way that origami artists use paper: They could fold, rather than cut and reseal, the material to create the best three-dimensional shape for storing water. That way there were no seams that could leak, and the container was strong enough to hold 120 gallons of water several feet off the ground. Besides avoiding the most basic problem of leakage, having the water-storage bag elevated a few feet was extremely useful, as it created enough pressure for a farmer to use a hose, not just buckets, to water plants. They renamed the product the "InfiniCan," and this product took off much more quickly than our original design. The bags now sell in Myanmar for less than $5 each.

And the story continues. One team sent a member to Myanmar to continue learning and explore ways to iterate on the design even further. She found ways to produce the water-storage bag with less material, cutting additional costs. Though her insights were promising, she left Myanmar before the product was fully ready to be sold to consumers, and for seven months no additional progress was made. Then, on May 2, 2008, Cyclone Nargis hit Myanmar.

The Category 4 cyclone caused massive damage and killed over one hundred thousand people. Whole villages were wiped out. Millions were left homeless and hungry. Suddenly, more people than ever lacked a source of clean drinking water. NGOs and other groups scrambled to find an inexpensive, strong, transportable water container to help solve this problem.

Thousands of InfiniCans were quickly manufactured and distributed along with water pumps and chlorination tablets—everything needed to access, purify, and store massive amounts of clean water. A package of equipment that cost $40 could provide clean drinking water for up to one thousand people per day. In just the first few weeks after the cyclone hit, over nine thousand InfiniCans were ordered. A few weeks later, five hundred units were being produced each day, and demand still outpaced supply. After years of inspiration, thought, experimentation, mistakes, design, and redesign, and the involvement of many different, diverse perspectives, this humble product had evolved to be able to help thousands upon thousands of individuals.

Redefining success not as a destination but as a way of operating, and committing to a process of creation and implementation that includes constant thoughtful iteration, can help avoid the kind of complacency that is so dangerous to continued growth. The most innovative teams try to get better every single day, whether they have already seemed to solve the problem at hand or not. They are the ones who will find the best solutions and continue to lead over time.

Build, test, learn, and rebuild—again and again. Commit to a process of continual iteration to produce your greatest work.

Drops Fill the Pot

There is a Swahili proverb, "Haba na haba, hujaza kibaba," that translates in English to "Little by little, the pot gets filled."

It is easy to dismiss small, persistent changes. But over time, these tiny improvements add up, and can result in the most significant and meaningful progress.

As I learned in my d.school classes, iterative design is a method of creating something new that is based on a process of building, testing, deciding what works and what doesn't, and fixing it (or building again from scratch). Slowly, a product or an idea is refined through this process, and with each change, the product improves. Each successive version is supposed to be a little bit better. Sometimes, it's a lot better.

Shona's designs did not come to her overnight. Sometimes the adjustments were as minor as replacing a pillow with a rolled-up blanket to help Shelly sit up straighter, and sometimes it meant building entirely new wheelchairs that looked unlike anything on the market, like ones with big, nubby wheels that could handle the rough off-road terrain in a typical village.

Why doesn't everyone make improvements this way, continuously testing, learning, adjusting, and getting better every day? Conventional wisdom tells us that a long, careful lead-up to a big launch of some new version of your product is best. Especially at larger organizations, we are often told to take our time and turn inward: to propose thorough but static plans, describing the changes we want to make at length; to explain in detail exactly what steps will need to take place to get there; to forecast what the effect these changes or a new version of a product will have on income, costs, cash flow—in short, to describe a future that we just can't know. Once we have the necessary research completed and approvals in place, only then are we given permission to develop our product, spending dozens or hundreds or thousands of hours getting it ready for launch, with minimal customer input along the way. And finally, when everything is polished and perfected, we are allowed to show the world our new and (theoretically) better solution.

This thinking is outdated and ineffective. After spending months or even years developing a new version of a product without soliciting enough customer feedback, companies make things that people don't want. Worse, they may have spent too many resources and gone too far down the wrong path to turn back, and the entire venture fails.

Shona, and other smart entrepreneurs like her, choose the path of constant, fast-paced iteration. It's true that this process can be messy and intimidating. Working through your ideas out loud, testing through trial and error with other people, and getting feedback live from the people you're trying to serve can make some people feel vulnerable. It's less scary to work in secret until you think you have things figured out, because if you get it wrong, no one else finds out. But it never occurred to Shona that needing to adjust her designs was some kind of failure; she would never use that language. To her, making changes along the way was, quite simply, the most obvious process she knew to improve and find the best solutions.

Every successful organization I've been a part of has mastered the process of iteration and created a culture where this kind of thinking infuses the work of every team member. In software and many other tech companies, it can be especially easy to operate this way; getting data and feedback on what is working (and what is not) is now easy, cheap, and relatively straightforward, and making changes is sometimes as fast as a few keystrokes. But all ventures can utilize these principles.

Kiva's first website was bare bones. We had an "About" section, a "Lend" section that included a handful of borrower profiles, and that was about it. We knew it was imperfect, but we just put it out there and got feedback to make it better each day. There have been countless incremental improvements to the site since then, made by dozens if not over a hundred people over time. Slowly, it became the robust, powerful platform it is today.

Great ideas and great products do not have to manifest themselves in one fell swoop. Many masterpieces are built over time by trial and error, by steps forward and backward, by constant iteration.

Li the Tailor

RIP THE SEAM

Beijing, China
2008

In the spring of 2008 I had just begun an assignment to write
case studies on women entrepreneurs for the Stanford GSB.
For my first round of interviews, I arrived in China to meet
with tech entrepreneurs throughout Zhong Guan Cun. The
area is a hub of entrepreneurial activity in the Haidian
District of Beijing, often referred to as China's Silicon Valley.

After several long days of interviews and work on the case
studies, it was Saturday—my one day off in Beijing before
flying to Shanghai. I wanted to visit a fabric market, and had
been told by a few people to make my way to an area called
Muxiyuan. I quickly got lost among the maze of stalls;
everywhere I turned was a dizzying array of colors and
textures. I wandered, soaking in the myriad hues.

One young woman in her mid-twenties stood out from
the other women and men in their stalls. While others sat
chatting with one another or trying to get my attention,
she had a look of complete concentration on her face, wholly
focused on the task at hand as she sat at her sewing machine.

She was surrounded by mountains of cloth, some of it folded precisely and stacked into perfect rectangles, some of it in rumpled heaps. She seemed to be putting some finishing touches on a gorgeous red and gold cheongsam, a long, fitted, traditional Chinese dress that shined and shimmered even here, in the middle of this windowless, fluorescent-lit storehouse. I was hypnotized.

I must have stared long and hard enough for her to have felt my presence. She stopped what she was doing, looked up, and asked me in a word, "American?" I blinked, and shook my head to snap out of my daze. "Yes. Sorry. How did you know?" She winked. "It's easy to tell," she replied.

We began to talk about the dress she was making. And then, because I couldn't help myself, I began to ask her questions about her work. How had she learned to sew like that? Was business good? Did she work with anyone else?

The young woman's name was Li. Her mother also sewed and had taught her everything she knew. As a girl Li would spend time watching her mother at work, marveling at the bright colors of the fabric and the magically delicate thread. Instead of needing outright instruction, Li picked up lots of little tricks along the way, like how to make the right kind of loops and knots to tie off the end of a stitch, how to stop the edges of torn cloth from fraying, how to sew a straight hem, and how to reinforce a seam.

Because Li's family struggled to make ends meet, she started to assist her mother in sewing projects early on. She found the work easy, and she was good at it, so over time it seemed only natural that she would sew as well. When her mother's eyesight failed and her hands grew weak and gnarled from arthritis, Li took over. She sold fabric, made custom-fit clothing, and did repairs. She not only used what her mother had taught her but built on it, incorporating her own style and ideas along the way.

Li told me all about her newest sewing machine, an electric one, which she had recently purchased. It was modern and shaped like something meant to race, quite the opposite of the ancient, elaborate manual sewing machine in the corner, with a huge hand wheel and a heavy foot pedal that looked like thick metal lace. There were other contrasts of the old and the new in her small stall: A worn measuring tape curled up next to shiny, razor-sharp scissors; yellowing pattern paper rested under an unopened plastic package of new needles, fanned out from smallest to largest in the container. Scraps and cuttings of fraying cloth had fallen to the floor beneath the machine, and untouched bolts of fabric were stacked neatly on the high shelves behind Li.

She knew how to fix almost any garment that needed fixing. To this end, perhaps more important than her skills at sewing two pieces of cloth together, Li was refreshingly unsentimental about the process of undoing her work and cutting things apart when necessary.

Li talked me through her basic steps to repair a garment. She knew that it was counterproductive to fight the nature of a fabric, so first she assessed that, taking note of how the thing was constructed. Sometimes a garment twists and pulls with wear, eventually becoming misshapen, because it hasn't been put together with consideration of the way the fabric itself has been woven. The warp, weft, and bias† of the cloth determine this, and cannot be changed. When something is sewn without regard to these three aspects, the fabric will stretch and pull, become more quickly worn, or even tear in unpredictable ways.

Li also knew to examine the garment from the inside out. As anyone who has sewn knows, stitching a shirt or a dress or

---

† Warp threads run lengthwise, creating the straight grain of the cloth, and make up the core of a fabric, giving it body and form. The weft threads fill in the rest of the fabric; they might be softer, or more colorful, complementing the warp threads to create its texture and design. The bias of a fabric runs 45 degrees diagonally from the straight grain. This is the stretchiest part on the fabric.

anything else with the wrong side out hides the messy parts of sewing: The seams, the cuts, the knots, the loose ends of thread, and even minor mistakes can hide tucked away, on the underside. Li always turned fabric inside out to really understand the problem.

Li knew that sometimes, even when a garment looked perfect, it wasn't—because it wasn't perfect for the person it was intended for. It no longer fit. The only way to fix it was to have the customer try the garment on so she could understand what needed to be taken in or let out. Li eagerly found even the tiniest details to adjust. The more she worked with the customers, the more she could find to fix, and the more tailored each item of clothing became.

Lastly, Li knew that sometimes, starting from scratch was the only way to fix a mistake. Good seamstresses and tailors know that removing a few stitches—or many stitches—may be the only way to repair a garment. Sometimes adding more fabric in certain places was necessary, but other times it meant cutting away the excess. Either of these things usually meant ripping seams and starting over. Learning to go back, undo, and redo stitches is a crucial skill for a seamstress if she wants to create the strongest, best-fitting, most beautiful clothes.

Li's wisdom has stayed with me.

You'll make fewer mistakes as a leader if you can avoid fighting your own nature or the nature of your team. Understand the fabric of your organization, be aware of the ongoing forces pulling on it or stretching it out in certain directions. Position yourself, and construct your team, accordingly.

You'll understand what went wrong more quickly and more thoroughly if you're willing to turn things inside out, so to speak. Don't tuck problems away to hide them. Reflect and look inside to get the best, most honest understanding of what's not working.

You'll become even stronger if you take feedback from others, and work with them to find what's not working for them.

Finally, even when it's painful, you will move ahead more quickly if you don't get too attached to what you've built when the results aren't right. Even if you've done the original "stitching," be willing to undo it. When you must, rip the seams and begin again.

CHAPTER 11

Show and Tell

Transparency Trumps Perfection

I'm often asked about the hardest moments in Kiva's journey. There have been many challenges along the way, but the spring of 2007 comes to my mind first.

At the time, Kiva was experiencing some major highs. In March, traffic to the site had surged after *New York Times* columnist and Kiva lender Nicholas Kristof visited a Kiva borrower in Kabul, Afghanistan, and then wrote about the experience. The article became the third most emailed article on the day it was published, and over $250,000 was loaned on the site within seventy-two hours. By summer 2007, the organization cleared $10 million in loans. Matt and I had just been on *Oprah*. We were thriving.

Then we were hit with one of our first real crises as an organization. Shelby Clark, a Kiva fellow stationed in Uganda to work with a Kiva field partner named WITEP (the Women's Initiative to Eradicate Poverty), reported that he was beginning to have doubts about the veracity of WITEP's work. He suspected that at least some of the money sent by Kiva lenders wasn't making it to the borrowers they had intended it for. Additionally, while he couldn't put his finger on exactly what was going on, he suspected that more than one of the staff there was hiding something from him. He just sensed that something was off. We encouraged him to stay quiet but observe carefully.

After weeks of detective work, Shelby discovered more than enough to confirm his initial suspicions. He found information proving that the leaders of the organization were indeed taking money for themselves instead of lending it to borrowers. As Shelby dug deeper, he uncovered many more lies. Most of the staff members were using fake names. Everyone had been lying to him on a daily basis. Many of the people listed as members of WITEP's board of directors did not even exist. Shelby discovered, piece by piece, that the entire organization was a façade, including the borrower profiles. In fact, he found two sets of loan agreements between Kiva and WITEP's borrowers—one set real and the other falsified. WITEP was one big scam.

While Shelby certainly took the brunt of the emotional trauma that came along with these discoveries, my heart broke as well. The group behind WITEP had taken advantage of Kiva lenders, and that hurt. We felt stupid for not having seen it coming. We felt embarrassed. But most painful was the realization that the man in charge, the person behind this grand scheme, was someone I thought I knew well, and whom I cared about deeply: Moses Onyango. This was the same Moses I'd met during my original trip to East Africa with Village Enterprise in 2004, and who had helped me find our first seven borrowers in 2005. This was the same Moses who had become my close friend. The Moses who had been like a brother to me. The Moses who had taken me to the church where he preached. I had lived in his home. I had shared meals with him and his family and spent hours playing with his kids. He had even named his son after Matt. The relationship had seemed to be as solid as they come. In fact, we had considered Moses our co-founder in Africa.

When Shelby shared all of his findings with us, we told the board what had happened and got to Uganda as fast as we could. I was there for the first few days and then Matt took over, assembling a team on the ground to help us fix what had happened. He spoke to Moses at length, but Moses had nothing to say about the nearly $125,000—half of the

$250,000 that had been raised for loans through WITEP—that he had siphoned away from borrowers. The money had disappeared.

We were devastated. Our most important relationship in East Africa was severed. And now we owed an explanation to hundreds of lenders. How were we going to tell them what had happened? We valued transparency, but until now we had only had happy things to be transparent about, or at worst, failures that were the result of something else positive like the site shutting down for a few hours because of its overwhelming popularity. Being open and transparent about those things was easy and fun. But being open and transparent about this case of fraud? This would not be so fun.

And yet there was no option other than to simply tell the truth. So we swallowed our pride and drafted an email to the affected WITEP lenders. We communicated the basics of what had happened and let them know that their funds had not made it to the borrowers. Then, because we had enough cash in the bank for our operational expenses and felt it was the right thing to do, we decided we would refund the lenders' money. (This was an exception to our policy of having lenders take on default risk, because this was Kiva's first case of fraud.) We read and reread the email, and finally, on August 22, 2007, we sent it to lenders, and we waited.

I anticipated angry responses. I had nightmares that reporters would be outside our door when we woke up, pushing microphones in our faces, demanding to know how we had been so stupid. I imagined the postman dragging huge bags of hate mail into the office.

But none of these things happened. The reaction from lenders was overwhelmingly positive. People were grateful that we had been honest. They felt that they were part of something real, something that was imperfect but improving every day. Our transparency made them even more trusting of Kiva. In fact, the vast majority of lenders turned around and re-loaned the money we had just returned to them.

There have been other cases of fraud since then, and the organization has handled each with the same spirit of openness and transparency. Every single case is posted on the Kiva site for anyone to see. For example, in the first few years, a partner in Côte d'Ivoire loaned $300 at a time to borrowers, but listed the loan sizes as $1,200 on the Kiva website. In Kenya, an executive director of one of Kiva's partner MFIs passed away, and her husband took funds to pay off his own debts. In Ecuador, a startup microfinance institution inflated loan sizes by 30 percent and used the extra money to fund its operational costs.

In each case of fraud, the organization had to take a hard look at what was working, and what was not. Sometimes we found elements of our process that were broken and we had to rip the seams, so to speak, to build something better. But regardless of how we fixed the situation, Kiva made sure everyone—our borrowers, our partners, the press—was told exactly how we had failed and why, and we placed information about these and all other cases of fraud on the Kiva site for anyone to see.

Today, the Kiva that Moses took advantage of doesn't exist anymore. Soon after that incident, Kiva developed an innovative five-star rating system to consider risk factors for each field partner. Other partnerships that led to cases of fraud were ones Matt and I brought on in the earliest days of Kiva's life, well before the organization had enough time or money to do intense due diligence or hire actual auditing firms, and they have since been shut down. Today the process of becoming a Kiva field partner is a rigorous one. Only those that make it through the lengthy, thorough application process are allowed to post loans on the website. Kiva has evolved into a stronger, smarter, more resilient organism that has vastly improved its process for finding, vetting, accepting, and managing partnerships around the world, and as a result, cases of fraud have been drastically reduced.

Mistakes still happen. But now, when they do happen, the organization is more committed than ever to transparency and to making whatever adjustments are necessary so that the same mistake doesn't happen twice.

Operating with radical transparency is difficult. It can make your organization feel vulnerable, which is scary, and it comes with some risk. But in my experience, it is not only the right thing to do, it is the most beneficial path for you and your organization in the long run.

Only by being honest about what is working and what isn't working can organizations find ways to improve, together. Transparency draws people in. It shows them that they are not on the outside, but on the inside, experiencing the journey with you. No one expects perfection, but everyone does (and should) demand honesty and will be inspired by resilience.

We all make mistakes. Admit it, fix it, do what you can to make sure those mistakes don't happen again in the future, and move on.

Find the Next Adventure

In the spring of 2013 I stood on the stage of a crowded auditorium in front of the toughest kind of audience I speak to. This wasn't a group of powerful CEOs—they don't intimidate me. It wasn't an international group, where I'd have to wait for translators to catch up, ruining the timing of pretty much all of my jokes. It wasn't a gathering of highly knowledgeable social entrepreneurs or development practitioners who had decades more experience and expertise than me.

These were high school students. They don't let you get away with anything.

I was speaking at a private boarding school in Massachusetts, and we had just begun the Q&A after I had given a brief lecture about microfinance, Kiva, and my journey as an entrepreneur. A petite girl in glasses stepped up to one of the microphones in the aisle. "Hi. I'm Sophie and I'm a freshman. So, my question is, if Kiva is so great, why didn't you just, like, stay there forever?"

I hesitated. I could give her the long answer, or the short one.

A few years after the incredible journey of Kiva began, I did something I never thought I'd do: I left the organization.

At the beginning, I had no intention of leaving. I thought I *would* stay at Kiva forever. The organization was growing at a breakneck pace and was recognized around the world. Oprah had been just the beginning. We were lauded as "the only nonprofit that matters" by CNN. We were praised as "one of the fastest-growing social benefit websites in history," as "revolutionary," as "world-changing," and more. We were inundated by positive press, awards, and recognition.

Professionally, I was in a wonderful place. Personally, though, I was not. The outside did not match the inside.

As Kiva grew and changed, so did I. The intensity of Kiva's first few frantic years took a huge toll on me and on my relationships. There were the typical, expected stresses that come with start-up life: lack of sleep, skipping meals and exercise, ignoring holidays, neglecting the needs of my family and friends. It was not a pretty picture. But in addition, there were other challenges around the fact that I was married to my co-founder, Matt.

Marriage can be tough at times. It is even harder when you are managing a rapidly growing start-up with your spouse. Work problems can follow you home, and conflict at home can bleed into work. The obligations of being a partner in a marriage sometimes conflict with the obligations of being a co-founder of a start-up. It's even harder than usual to protect any semblance of work-life balance. Personal time blurs with work time. Does it count as date night if you both want to stay at the office and finish a project together? What if only one of you wants to stay and one wants to go? Does that mean one cares about the company more—and the other about the marriage more? What if decisions like this must be faced every single day, for years on end?

When only one member of a couple is tired and stressed all the time from start-up life, the other half can buffer some of that anxiety, help shoulder the burden, and balance out the energy level. But when both people are in this state constantly, no one has the vantage point to suggest a broader perspective. When you are working with your significant other and your start-up is taking off, you might feel immeasurable pressure to take advantage of this once-in-a-lifetime opportunity—and some days you might disagree on whether or not the more pressing, once-in-a-lifetime opportunity needing your attention is the start-up or the marriage.

I'm sure that some relationships thrive under shared pressure; the nonstop hours and shared stress might even bring certain couples closer together. For a long time I believed that that could be—or even should be—us. But it was not. To be clear, the pressure of growing Kiva is not the sole reason Matt and I ended up eventually separating. Like any couple, we had our own unique mix of strengths and weaknesses. It would be unfair (and impossible) to attempt to summarize the entire relationship here. What's important to know is that, at the end of the day, our relationship ultimately buckled under the weight of those weaknesses.

As it sunk in that our relationship was in real trouble, it occurred to me that separating from Matt meant risking a separation from Kiva too. Though I didn't want that to happen, in the end I felt I had no choice. I had to consider what was best for me in my personal life apart from what might be best for me at work. It would have been wrong to stay in an unhappy relationship just because I loved Kiva. And I would have gladly walked away from Kiva if I believed doing so would have solved our marriage problems—but that would not have worked either.

So Matt and I began the process of separating. I moved out. But we still saw each other in the office every day. I decided to create breathing room for both of us, volunteering to work from home for a while. That helped, but it also hurt. I had no daily, face-to-face contact with my team. Distance created more distance. Soon I felt removed not just from Matt, but from what was happening at work. Yet it seemed almost impossible to reverse our roles at that point, to have Matt work from home instead of me. A precedent had been set. I felt deep regret; I had accidentally given away much more than I had intended, and now it seemed like there was no going back. I realized that the distance I had created, even though it was intended to help both of us and to be only a temporary arrangement, would be nearly impossible to close.

After a few months of feeling increasingly disconnected and disengaged, I realized I had to make a clear choice about the future. I could fight my way back in to Kiva and demand to work full-time again in the office, or I could keep taking steps away. For a variety of reasons, I did not fight. At the time, it seemed impossible for both Matt and me to stay at Kiva, and I did not want to "split the baby" and harm the organization by arguing any more about it. At that moment, taking a break from the beautiful thing that Matt and I had created together felt like the best way to care for it.

It was the hardest thing I've ever done. Separating from a marriage and a start-up at the same time felt like a double amputation that had been partially self-inflicted, and partially beyond my control. Some days I felt like both a victim and a fool. My sense of identity dissolved, and I was suddenly cut off from the relationships, the role, and the community that had come to define me. For months I felt lost. I felt alone. I felt angry.

Eventually, though, I would come to be grateful for the sequence of events that pulled me away from Kiva. The clean break from an old life gave me the chance to build a new one, one in which I could reclaim my sanity, reestablish my sense of self, and carve out room to grow in new ways. When I glimpsed this, I was able to choose and even embrace the path before me. I was able to get genuinely excited about what my future might hold. Leaving Kiva at that moment in time turned out to be the best thing that could have happened.

So when Sophie, the freshman standing at the microphone, asked me that day why I'd left, I replied with a smile and told her, "It was time to go find the next adventure."

That's the short version of my answer. But it's the most important part of the long version. In the middle of a painful transition, I made a choice: I chose to believe that there would be another adventure on the other side.

Abasi the Farmer

HARNESS THE STORM

Outside Kigali, Rwanda
2007

Abasi, a farmer I met in Rwanda, was obsessed with watching the weather. He was a bit of an armchair meteorologist. He talked at length about the changing of the seasons and what it meant for growing cycles. He had an intimate and almost intuitive understanding of what an unusually hot day or a sudden cool breeze or heavy clouds above meant for his crops. He knew how to time planting and harvesting around rainy and dry seasons. He patiently explained to me his many strategies for managing severe rains, from propping up an old oil drum so he could harvest rainwater off his roof to digging extra ditches around his crops in order to direct the runoff water away from his seedlings.

However, all of this knowledge still did not give him complete control. Sometimes all he could do was wait, watch, and withstand the elements as best he could. Other times, he knew that waiting for the right season to come along to plant was smarter than beginning at the wrong time and losing everything to a drought or a downpour.

Experienced farmers do not look at their fields and see a static picture. They see an ever-changing, multidimensional landscape that is subject to the sun, the shade, the winds, the rain, and the dry spells. They have a dynamic understanding of how the broader environment can affect their crops. This perspective helps them anticipate changes, protect themselves from sudden threats, and take advantage of positive trends.

Likewise, smart entrepreneurs recognize the forces around them that they cannot control—especially those forces that can hinder their progress—and they plan for them the best they can. They manage the inevitable storms so minimal damage will occur. When a downpour is imminent, they are thoughtful and proactive. They make plans to channel the rainwater and, whenever possible, to harness the power of the storm to achieve the best outcome.

CHAPTER 12

Master the Art of Reinvention

Inspired Again

Elizabeth Gilbert's bestselling book *Eat Pray Love*, which chronicles her journeys around the world after her divorce, was published just before my own marriage to Matt ended. A number of friends passed along copies to me. Needless to say, I felt obligated to read it.

The book reflected a lot of what I was feeling and experiencing. Soon after separating from Matt and subsequently leaving Kiva, I decided to travel for a few months. Instead of roaming around as I'd expected I would do, I ended up living in one place—one very beautiful place, in the beach house of good friends in Mexico. I packed one suitcase full of books and journals, and along with my surfboard, threw a yoga mat and a handful of clothes into my enormous surfboard carrier. That was it. This would be my way of recalibrating. Instead of doing the "eat, pray, love" sequence I was more on a "sleep, surf, write" sort of schedule. After years of all-nighters, all work, and no time for reflection, I prioritized sleep, spent hours a day in the ocean, and wrote. (It was during my time in Mexico, actually, that I began this book.)

I began to heal. Physically, I grew stronger every day, thanks to hours of surfing, hiking, yoga, and walking wherever I could. Emotionally, I felt like I had gone through a rebirth. Spiritually, I found a new intimacy with God and basked in a spirit of love, forgiveness, and peace that I had never experienced before. Professionally, as I took stock of my situation, I mourned what I had given up. I had no job. I had no immediate prospects. I didn't even have an updated résumé; my most recent one was from before business school. But as I had learned so many times before, I knew not to keep score by anyone else's calculations. I knew I was in charge of deciding what mattered to me, and measuring my success based on that. I had become crystal clear about what I valued, and had chosen a path that would allow me to rebuild a life around those values.

Then, after I had been in Mexico a few months, an opportunity came to me. During the few minutes each day I hopped online to check my email, I found a note from one of my favorite Stanford GSB Professors, Garth Saloner. I had gotten to know him most when he and his daughter Romy came on a service-learning trip to Uganda that I had organized while in business school. Along with a dozen of my classmates, we had traveled together, visited Kiva entrepreneurs, and talked about microfinance and development over the course of a week in East Africa.

Professor Saloner was now dean of the business school, and he was passing along news about a full-time open position in the GSB's case-writing office. It was an opportunity to work for ten months writing case studies on women entrepreneurs in developing and emerging markets. Goldman Sachs's 10,000 Women initiative would fund the work, and I would have the incredible opportunity to travel all over the world to do research and interviews with the entrepreneurs.

I pursued the opportunity immediately. As soon as I found out I had won the position, I flew back from Mexico to begin my new work. I knew that this was now what I needed even more than the blissful, quiet routine I had fallen into: to get back out into the field, among my favorite kind of people in the world—entrepreneurs!

Over most of the next year, I worked with the Acumen Fund, Endeavor, and other organizations that invested funding or resources (or both) in entrepreneurs all around the world. These organizations helped me identify a few dozen individuals who might be good candidates for case studies. I did research online, made some phone calls, and created a short list of people to interview. Then, just weeks after I returned home from Mexico, I packed again and began an almost nonstop journey to a dozen different countries to interview these entrepreneurs. I met a wide variety of truly inspiring women, from Shona, the wheelchair designer in South Africa, to Zica, the hair-salon mogul in Brazil, to the CEO of a tech start-up in Jordan to a jewelry maker in Egypt to an owner of skin-care centers in Lebanon, and many more.

Despite the diversity of backgrounds, industries, and cultures, I saw more similarities in these women than differences. They were creative. They were optimists. They were incredibly driven. They were courageous. None had taken no for an answer. Collectively, they had overcome almost every kind of obstacle one could imagine. And while each person manifested it in a unique way, an unmistakable entrepreneurial spirit shone bright in every single one of them.

I found myself thinking about these women and their lives long after my research and interviews with them were over. They had lodged themselves in my heart, alongside countless others whom I had met over the previous years through Kiva and my work with Village Enterprise. The entrepreneurs I met, whether poor farmers or college-educated execs, shared an entrepreneurial spirit that was contagious. They were fighters, the kind of people who figured out how to pursue what they wanted no matter what and how to go over, around, or through whatever barriers stood in their way. Despite their difficult circumstances, they chose to act. It seemed like nothing could keep them down. They embodied hope.

More than ever before, they were who I wanted to be.

I had come full circle since my early days as a temp at Stanford nearly seven years earlier. I knew by now that my old black-and-white ideas about a world in which entrepreneurs were the selfish ones, focused only on money, and nonprofit folks were the saints, focused only on impact, were wrong. I had become convinced once again that great entrepreneurs can be great forces for good in the world, and are often masters of empathy, service, and generosity.

In fact, the most inspiring entrepreneurs I have met are unapologetically focused on, if not obsessed with, serving others. They want to make the world better for as many people as possible. They have chosen an entrepreneurial path so they can be a force for positive change in other people's lives. They have chosen to live an entrepreneurial life because they believe it can be a path of service. They have trained themselves to see other people's problems, to frame those problems as opportunities, and to work in a disciplined way to solve them and create value for others. They define value broadly, not just in terms of a financial reward, and believe that it should be spread to as many people as possible—not just to paying customers. These kind of entrepreneurs often call themselves "social entrepreneurs," but sometimes they don't care to label themselves at all; they simply express who they are through what they do and how they do it.

Through those interviews with strong women all over the world, I became convinced once more that living entrepreneurially was not just still an option for me, it was the only option. Leaving Kiva did not mean I had given up the chance to be an entrepreneur; on the contrary, I was now free to revitalize my own entrepreneurial spirit and direct my energies toward a new goal. Each woman I met along the way that year after I left Mexico was living proof of this. They could not have known it, but simply by sharing their stories of their own entrepreneurial journeys with me, they breathed life back into mine.

ProFounder

At the end of my assignment, I was back at the Stanford GSB, handing in my final case studies to Dean Saloner. It was my last day of work for the 10,000 Women project.

As I was leaving, lugging a box of office supplies, I bumped into my friend and fellow GSB alumna Dana Mauriello. She asked what I was up to, and I motioned toward the box and told her it was my last day of work at the GSB—and therefore, I said, my first day of something else. What that something else was, I didn't know. But I told Dana I hoped to gather a team and start something again soon. I was not yet sure what that start-up would be, but I knew I wanted to continue creating tools to empower entrepreneurs. Except that this time, after all my travels, I wanted to build something here at home in the United States, for entrepreneurs in my own backyard. As I shared this with Dana, she nodded excitedly in agreement and told me that empowering entrepreneurs was her passion too. In fact for the last several months she had been piloting her own venture, a key element of which included equipping entrepreneurial people around the world to find and promote important trends they observed in the fashion and beauty industry.

Dana and I kept talking. And we kept talking. Not just that day, but the following day, and the next, and the next. We heard ourselves ask the same questions over and over again to one another: Have you ever wanted to invest in a local small business you love? Have you wished you could own stock in your friend's promising start-up? Have you ever dreamed of starting your own venture, funding it with the help of friends and family—or even going beyond your own network to crowdfund, collecting financial support from anyone in the general public who might want to invest? We wanted to do all of these things, but we didn't know how to make them happen.

At the time, doing any of the above was, at best, a confusing, awkward, and expensive process. At worst it was impossible, because laws limited the number of people (specifically, people who aren't wealthy, "accredited" investors) who could invest in a private enterprise. Some states allow hundreds of unaccredited investors to participate, but some allow only a handful. Some states choose to have their restrictions apply not only to investors within their state but nationally, which means that other investors living in more lenient states must also comply by the stricter state's laws. For example, if you wanted to have an unaccredited investor from Connecticut invest in your business, you could only have nine other unaccredited investors contribute—so, ten people total. Not just ten from Connecticut, but ten nationally. And not just for this round of fund-raising, but for the lifetime of your business.

So a lot of entrepreneurs just raised money off the books, illegally, offline, in conversations with friends and family members that often ended awkwardly and without clear expectations set on the exact terms of the investment. But for entrepreneurs who wanted to do this legally, they had to go to lawyers and accountants who, of course, would charge handsomely for their services.

A few months later, Dana and I, along with another classmate, Evan Reas, began working on ProFounder in an attempt to solve some of these problems. We wanted to allow start-ups and small businesses to raise investment funds from their friends, family, and community members for very little cost. ProFounder, a for-profit company, was one of the earliest attempts to push securities-based crowdfunding forward in the United States. We offered users a host of different tools: They could utilize our legal compliance engine to quickly and easily research state and federal laws related to their start-ups, and even complete necessary forms online; they could develop a pitch and corresponding website for their business's fund-raising campaign; they could instantly create term sheets based on either equity or revenue share by answering a few quick questions; and they could manage and communicate with investors, among much else. In essence, what we built was as much of a full service, start-to-finish, collaborative crowdfunding platform for online investments as we could create at the time, given that actual securities-based crowdfunding was still illegal.

It took a year to research all of the legal restrictions in each U.S. state and to build the software we needed to get ProFounder up and running. Evan ended up stepping away from the company before the site went live, but Dana and I pressed on to launch. Within a few months after the site was up, we had already helped dozens of entrepreneurs raise funding for a wide variety of different ventures, including Uncle Clay's candy store in Honolulu, a shoe company in Chicago, an electric motorcycle company in San Francisco, CiCi's whale-watching and ecotourism business in San Diego, a brewery in Fargo, a coffee roasting company in Denver, and many more.

ProFounder was off to a promising start!

Sarah the Chicken Farmer

COUNT WHAT MATTERS

Outside Accra, Ghana
2007

I met Sarah a few weeks after I graduated from Stanford's
Graduate School of Business with my newly minted master of
business administration, and, like so many newly minted
MBA grads, I felt I knew everything. Or at least a lot of things.
About business, anyway.

Perhaps I felt especially proud because my path to becoming
an MBA student had been a nontraditional one. By most
measures I had not been an obvious business school candidate.
I had a liberal arts background, not one in business or finance
or accounting. My Stanford GSB application essay had been
atypical, to say the least; in answer to the question "What
Matters to You Most, and Why?" I wrote a long-form poem
about finding one's voice in the world. Later in the application
process, during an interview with a GSB alumnus, I admitted I
had never used Excel but gushed about recently learning to
speak Swahili. I had a great deal of nonprofit and volunteer
experience, having spent years in developing countries
working on ways to alleviate poverty, but the closest to any

business experience I had, besides a paper route when I was twelve, were a couple of summer jobs during high school: one as an art instructor in a tiny studio in my hometown, another as a waitress at the Ground Round, a goofy family restaurant that showed old-timey silent cartoons on a big screen and served popcorn instead of bread.

Armed with this miscellany of knowledge and experiences, I strode onto campus for my first day of business school ready to take on the world. But then classes started.

I found my accounting class to be particularly challenging. It was the very first class of my MBA program, and it was held at 8 A.M. Most students were still waking up at that hour; we clutched our life-giving cups of coffee throughout class. I didn't have too much trouble staying awake because class was one big, ongoing surprise. My initial reaction when we walked through the syllabus on the first day was to laugh in bewilderment. What were these concepts anyway? Double-entry bookkeeping systems (I thought double counting was a bad thing!), cash versus accrual accounting (people still used cash?), FIFO and LIFO (*Dr. Seuss* characters?), and many other suspicious terms kept me entertained and on my toes.

When all was said and done, thanks to my two (yes, two) accounting tutors, an incredible study group, and a lot of hard work, I passed the class. And I'd like to think I took away the important, big-picture concepts from it, if not all of the details. For instance, I became convinced that, much to my surprise, accounting is an art. As with many other seemingly straight-forward processes, nuances abound, and strategic decisions must be made along the way. I learned that a list of numbers on a page can tell a rich story about the life of a business, whether in balance-sheet snapshots or over time through income statements. I learned how information helps us understand the health of an organization. What matters most is knowing what you need to count, and then designing the best system for keeping track of everything.

By the end of that class, I had learned a lot. By the end of my MBA program, having seen those basic accounting principles applied in a variety of case studies throughout the rest of the curriculum, I had learned even more. It had taken me two years, but I left Stanford with a respectable comprehension of accounting principles and how to apply them in a variety of situations.

Then, a few weeks after I graduated and was off to new adventures, I met Sarah in Ghana. It took only a few minutes with her to cut to the heart of what accounting is really about.

I was in Ghana conducting research and due diligence on a microfinance institution that had provided Sarah with a small loan, and I had just finished a tour of her chicken coop, a tiny structure next to her house, in a rural area outside Accra. The coop was muggy and dark, a cacophony of clucks and squawks and the sound of chicken feet scratching and shuffling across the dirt floor. It was so small that I was halfway bent over throughout the tour, angled directly above the panicked birds, constantly worried about where I stepped. Their sudden flaps would send quick, scattered little gusts of air whirling up to my face, tossing dust and feathers into my eyes and nose. Even after the tour was over and we emerged from the coop into the daylight, my eyes still watered. I couldn't stop sneezing. Yet Sarah's exuberance and pride over her young chickens made it all a joyful experience.

Sarah led me inside her small home adjacent to the coop. There she offered me tea and fruit and gestured for me to take a seat on a green plastic lawn chair whose main design benefit was its ability to stack easily with other chairs, though Sarah owned only one. The chair was flimsy and bowed when I sat down; its legs wobbled when I shifted my weight or crossed or uncrossed my legs. I sat as still as I could.

As Sarah cleared off a tiny wooden table to make room for our tea, I noticed two shelves on the wall, each with teacups perched upon it. The upper shelf held six cups, all of them matching and looking quite new. Sarah pulled two down and poured our tea into them. The lower shelf held maybe two dozen cups. While this might seem normal for someone in America, where there seems to exist a widespread, irresistible tendency to hoard coffee mugs, two dozen or so cups seemed to be quite a lot for someone with relatively few possessions. What was more, the lower shelf's cups were old and chipped. Some were so badly cracked that they looked unusable. They were arranged oddly as well—some were stacked one inside another, some were upright, others overturned—whereas the teacups on the top shelf were lined up in a perfect row. Maybe these cups had sentimental value? Maybe she found broken cups to repair and resell? I made a mental note to ask her about it later. But first, we needed to talk about her business. Our conversation went something like this:

I asked: "How many chickens do you have?"

Sarah: "I have the ones we just saw."

Me: "What are your plans for them?"

Sarah: "They will grow and then I will sell them at the market."

Me: "Of course. How much will you sell each chicken for?"

Sarah: "It depends on when we go to the market. And it depends on which kind I sell."

Me: "Well, how much would you need to make a good profit?"

Sarah: "I will ask for enough."

Me: "What is enough? In the beginning, how much did you spend on these chickens as chicks?"

Sarah: "I traded some bags of maize."

Me: "What was the value of that maize?"

Sarah: "It was worth these chicks. Or maybe a little bit less."

Me, getting a little frustrated that she seemed to be avoiding my questions: "Okay, let me ask you this another way. Since you bought the chicks, how much has it cost you to feed them and care for them? How much do you think you have spent on them from the beginning until now?"

Sarah sighed and looked at me with what appeared to be pity. It seemed sad to her that I was so dense, that it was so difficult for me to understand simple things.

Sarah: "Every day I have not spent too much."

Me: "Yes, but how do you keep track of your revenue and your costs—the money that comes in and the money that goes out? How do you measure? Do you keep records?"

Somewhat exasperated, Sarah got up and pointed to the teacups on the lower shelf.

"Here," she said. She picked up a big mug and dipped it into a bag of chicken feed that sat below the shelves. She scooped up some feed, then dumped it back in the bag. Then she put the cup back in its place and moved one of the smaller cups to the far end of the shelf. She paused, looked back at me to see if I comprehended, and then moved it back again to its original spot.

"I move these cups. When they are all over here, I take some chickens to the market. Then I have money. Then I buy more food. Sometimes I buy other things too."

Sarah could not read or write. She certainly had never taken a single accounting class. But she had developed her own system—*an abacus made from old teacups*—to manage her inventory. I knew her patience for me on this topic was waning, so after she showed me that not just the position of the cups mattered but that overturned cups meant one thing and right-side-up cups meant another, I nodded, took some notes, and said we could move on.

Stepping away from her teacups, she summarized, with a sense of pride: "All the time I keep getting more chickens, and selling more chickens, and I can buy more food for them and for my family. My activities are growing."

While I'm not sure I fully grasped every detail of Sarah's teacup system, it worked for her. By virtue of the fact that she had kept her business alive over time, she knew how to measure what was meaningful to her and she knew how to stay profitable enough to survive. She had been in business for years, beginning with only a few chicks that fit into a single box; clearly she was balancing what she spent and what she earned well enough to slowly grow the number of chickens she owned over time.

Though Sarah did not know how to express it in the ways I had learned at Stanford, she knew exactly how to keep track of what she needed for her business to thrive. She had created her own means of measuring what was coming in and what was going out, and more often than not she found ways to make sure more was coming in.

The actual numbers weren't the point. The system itself wasn't the point. The point was staying in balance. Bringing in more than she used. Spending less than she made. Supporting her family while slowly but surely growing her business. These were her goals, and her tiny business was helping her achieve them.

She did not know formal accounting, but she was smart and had figured out how to measure what was meaningful to her. She had figured things out for herself, counting what mattered and ignoring what did not.

CHAPTER 13

The Goal May Not Be the Summit

When to Turn Back

ProFounder grew steadily for more than a year. We learned more and more about our customers every day, and we constantly improved our software. And slowly we realized that while we believed our technology offered the best solution at the time to the problems we aimed to fix, it wasn't perfect. It still wasn't what we really wanted to offer our customers. For instance, for legal reasons, entrepreneurs couldn't openly advertise that they were raising money online; they could only reach out to people they already knew. They couldn't crowdfund, soliciting anyone in the world for their support. In this and other ways, the legal landscape prohibited us from building a truly open, collaborative product.

So, three years after we began, we chose to shut ProFounder down.

Most people viewed ProFounder's shutdown in one of two ways. Fellow entrepreneurs, or others who followed crowdfunding trends closely, saw us as folks who had been on the front lines, who had fought the good fight, our chance at greater success taken away by the big, bad government. The people who believed this would pat us on the back and say things like, "You are crowdfunding pioneers who made it easier for the rest of us to follow. You took one for the team." The most extreme supporters saw our journey as a triumphant, sacrificial one. In their eyes, we had gotten as far as we could before legal limitations made it too dangerous to continue, but in doing so we had paved the way for others to follow us. This alone, some argued, meant that ProFounder had been a big victory for the crowdfunding industry.

Others saw ProFounder as a clear failure. In their eyes, any company that raised funding (as we had) and failed to provide investors with a way to cash out and get a financial return, through some liquidity event like an acquisition or IPO, was a failure, plain and simple. It's true: If success is measured solely on financial return, then yes, ProFounder failed.

But neither of these views felt quite right to me; neither one told the complete story. It took me several years to be able to articulate why I believe this is true. Specifically, I had a revelation in the spring of 2014, two years after ProFounder shut down. At the time, I was sitting in a classroom at the Harvard Kennedy School. It was the final day of an executive education program on leadership, and our class discussion revolved around case studies we had read about several epic journeys. The most popular case study seemed to be the one about the famous 1996 Mount Everest disaster, when eight climbers were killed and several others were stranded by a rogue storm. This case served as a springboard for a discussion about risk-taking, strategy, and goal-setting.

The Everest climbers were willing to take great risks in order to reach their goal, which was, obviously, to summit the mountain.

Or was it?

Our class dissected every detail we were given about the endeavor. We read individual accounts of what happened and tried to understand why the outcomes had been so different for people faced with the same set of choices in the same situation. Some made it home alive and others did not. Why? We came up with a startling hypothesis: Those who had survived knew that their goal was *not* to reach the top of a mountain, but to make it back down the mountain safely. So even when they were only a few hundred yards from the top of the mountain, when they saw the storm coming, they turned around before conditions got worse and made their way back down the mountain. It wasn't that they didn't care about the summit. They cared deeply about making it to the top; they had dedicated years of their lives and countless resources toward that goal. But they cared more about surviving, and as difficult and costly as the journey had been, when conditions worsened, they sacrificed the goal of reaching the summit to prioritize the goal of survival. Others, on the other hand, pushed ahead to get to the top of the mountain despite the approaching storm, and never made it down the mountain alive.

I realize that a few hours studying the Everest disaster inside a warm, safe classroom did not make me an expert on exactly what happened that day on the mountain. And no one can know exactly what decision-making process occurred within the minds of each member of the expedition during that fateful climb in 1996. But the hypothesis we came up with resonated with me deeply, as I believe the decision to shut down ProFounder shares some important similarities.

ProFounder's vision was an ambitious one. We chose to walk a path that few had walked before us, embarking on a journey that, in its own way, was fraught with barriers and risks. Yet over the first year or so of ProFounder's life, we did well. We were gaining traction. We were making progress. It looked as if we really might be able to build a big, successful venture that made it easy for anyone to raise investment capital. In other words, it looked like we might reach our own version of the summit.

And then, storms began to brew on the horizon. Lawmakers began to pay more attention to what we were doing, and this had both positive and negative consequences for us. ProFounder exposed the process of investment fund-raising for what it was (complicated, restrictive, and expensive), gave people full information and knowledge, and equipped them with what they needed to take full advantage of existing laws. Regulators, apparently, did not appreciate this. We had given people the tools to tiptoe right up to the edges of what the laws allowed, and I believe this newly informed constituency threatened the regulators. They certainly did not like being asked questions they could not answer—or, more accurately, questions that no one could yet answer. For example, many states limit not only the number of unaccredited investors but also have restrictions on whether "unsophisticated" investors can invest or not. What in the world does it mean, legally speaking, to be "sophisticated" or not? There is no clear answer. According to a *Wall Street Journal* MarketWatch article, sophistication is "both a legal distinction and a commonly used description, both of which are subject to interpretation." No one can take a test, pass, and officially become a "sophisticated" investor. But you and the company in which you've invested can get into trouble if you are found not to be sophisticated. Clear as mud.

Another boundary lacking definition and clarity, and perhaps a boundary ProFounder pushed that ruffled the feathers of state regulators the most, is the line between what is considered private and what is public in the fund-raising world. Big companies "go public" when they issue an IPO (initial public offering) on the stock market. This allows them to sell equity ownership in their company and access a huge new source of capital from the public. So what are private raises? A small business isn't going to become a public company and sell its stock on the stock market; the process of doing this is lengthy and expensive, and requires a great deal of information disclosure. It's just not a fit for most small companies. So instead of selling stock to the general public, smaller companies—most companies—do private raises. Because a raise is private, there are rules about how news of the opportunity is shared, and to whom. An entrepreneur whose start-up is raising funds privately cannot broadcast the opportunity publicly on a TV commercial or billboard. Instead she is more or less limited to seeking funds from people she already knows, or those with whom she has a "pre-existing, substantive relationship," commonly referred to as "friends and family." Again, there is a lot to question here. Do Facebook friends count? Are Twitter followers "friends" who qualify? No one had answered these questions.

At one point, California's Department of Corporations (DoC) approached us, concerned about the way we were defining some of these terms. Or, rather, they had questions about the way we were giving our customers full information (though not legal advice) and letting them define terms for themselves. Over the weeks and months that followed, we spent an unfortunate and frustrating amount of time educating the California DoC and responding to their questions about how our business operated and why we felt justified in defining things the way we had. We paid for many hours of legal research to be done and for official memos to be written to provide more robust answers to their questions. We did this to protect ourselves and preempt any sort of action against us. But no matter how much information we provided, it seemed they always needed more.

We felt frustrated not only by their lack of relevant knowledge but also by how this new ongoing dialogue slowed us down. We could no longer experiment and iterate as freely as we had been; the DoC was now watching our every move like a hawk, so we felt less able to try new things or take important risks. Every decision to push on a certain definition or boundary now had potential consequences at each turn. And our new relationship with the DoC meant that acting first and asking for forgiveness later wasn't an option. Because now that we had a more "collaborative relationship" with the DoC, we were more or less beholden to run each slightly risky or innovative idea by them first to see what they thought—and, then, even if it took months, to wait for their approval.

On top of this, our current product was not meeting the most important needs of our customers. While we knew we had made the process of raising investment capital from friends and family as simple and straightforward as possible, it still wasn't simple enough. It became clear to us that only if the laws changed would it be possible to create a superior product. Meanwhile, our bank accounts were getting smaller. Oh, and I was weeks away from giving birth to twins, becoming a mom for the first time.

This combination of factors was our approaching storm.

We had no lack of support. The world really seemed to be waking up to the enormous potential of crowdfunding, and we continued to gain accolades in the press. Many of our investors encouraged us to keep going, and offered to put even more money into the company. The passage of new legislation opening up the potential for legal, investment-based crowdfunding looked imminent. But we still had major doubts.

We did not feel that raising another large round was the most responsible thing to do, given the increasing number of factors related to our business that we could not control. We had become all too familiar with the regulatory environment, and given the pace of change, we knew we still wouldn't be able to offer what our customers truly wanted anytime soon.

On the most personal note, I knew that new motherhood to twins was going to be the biggest, most all-consuming adventure of my life. With the imminent arrival of two tiny babies, I wanted to be sure I could dedicate myself fully to them and their first few weeks and months. In the early days, I knew that I wanted to be present and personally available to them for whatever they needed. This was something I had communicated to my investors and to my team from the moment I knew I was pregnant.

All in all, there were too many unknowns. So Dana and I decided that the most responsible decision was to stop where we were and turn back.

We delivered the news to our small team and walked through the shutdown plan. Salaries stopped. We moved out of our office and sold the rest of our furniture. We began working with lawyers to officially wind down the company. But we had a few more things to do before we finally wrapped things up. We did not want to turn back without first trying to make the path better for future climbers.

We redirected our day-to-day efforts to support brand-new draft legislation, the JOBS Act, through Congress. The legislation would, among other things, allow entrepreneurs to raise up to a million dollars for their start-ups and small businesses from any—and as many—investors as they wished. We believed that pushing this legislation forward was where we could have the greatest impact in crowdfunding, in a way that was aligned with the core values of ProFounder. Dana testified before Congress several times about the promises of crowdfunding. Meanwhile I (too pregnant to fly) answered questions for reporters over the phone, and spoke at West Coast–based events about the promise of the Jumpstart Our Business (JOBS) Act. Dana also spoke at numerous venues about ProFounder's vision and progress, providing persuasive, inspiring arguments and real examples of entrepreneurs who had been able to harness the power of their communities to launch their ventures. We consulted regularly with lawmakers on crowdfunding, and even got to contribute to the language used in Title IV of the JOBS Act legislation.

In the end, thanks to input from us and a host of other entrepreneurs and concerned citizens, and thanks to a Congress that put aside its differences to get something done quickly, the JOBS Act became law. Our reward was an invitation to the White House to see the bill signed into law.

On April 5, 2012, I sat in a front-row seat among friends and colleagues in the White House Rose Garden and listened as President Obama addressed the small crowd: "One of the great things about America is that we are a nation of doers—not just talkers, but doers," he said. "We think big. We take risks. And we believe that anyone with a solid plan and a willingness to work hard can turn even the most improbable idea into a successful business. . . . That's the promise of America. That's what this country is all about."

The President made his way from the podium onstage to a desk beside it and picked up the first of more than a dozen pens lined up in a row on the desk next to him. He held the pen up, smiled, touched it to the paper, made a very small stroke, then stopped and put the pen back in its place next to the others. He picked up the second pen, marked another letter on the paper, and then promptly retired that pen to its place in the line-up on the table next to the first. This continued, pen after pen, letter after letter, until his name on the JOBS Act had officially signed it into law. The crowd stood, cheering and applauding. Dana and I hugged and cried. We couldn't have been prouder to see this historic event take place. It had been a long journey. ProFounder had officially closed its doors just weeks earlier. And I had given birth to two beautiful baby boys, who were healthy and thriving. The world was changing before our eyes.

Dana and I are proud of the impact ProFounder created, especially in the help we provided to start-up ventures and small businesses across the country. We are also grateful to have had a role influencing crowdfunding regulatory reform in Washington, and have cheered on other entrepreneurs who have picked up where we left off. It's been gratifying to know that we helped start a broader conversation.

I think even our investors, who lost money, would say that their experience with ProFounder was positive. Together, we all took a bet and conducted a set of experiments, and we all learned important lessons about the emerging opportunity of for-profit, investment-based crowdfunding. Those insights have shaped decisions about how some of our former investors have made other investments, and they continue to inform the path of new and emerging organizations trying to pick up where ProFounder left off. What ProFounder created has lived on, as our technology, assets, and expertise have been used by several of our investors and their organizations. All that said, we did not provide a financial payoff to our investors, and I wish we had been able to do that too. They took a chance on us, and despite all the good things ProFounder made happen in the world, I'm sure all of them would also have preferred a profitable exit as well.

At the end of the day, I know that we were right to turn back when we did. I have seen too many entrepreneurs get caught up in thinking that the goal of their efforts is to pursue their "summit"—usually a big financial exit—at any cost, personal or professional. Some do it, and have great stories to tell about narrowly escaping a storm. But countless others pay too great a price. They destroy relationships, do permanent damage to their health, waste millions of dollars, and push everyone around them to the brink. ProFounder's storms were real, and we had to make a choice. We chose to turn back.

Fatuma the Charcoal Seller

UNEARTH YOUR COINS

A village a few hours north of Dodoma, Tanzania
2004

Fatuma kept written records of her charcoal business. She
wanted to show me. She picked up a tiny stub of a pencil and
sharpened it with a small knife. Then she opened up one of a
dozen or so of the flimsy blue books she kept in a pile—they
looked like the same kind of official blue books I had used to
write my midterm essays as an undergraduate—to point out
yesterday's numbers, and let me watch her make note of
today's sales.

I was genuinely impressed as she walked me through her
meticulously kept records. We discussed the previous few
months and the profits her business had made. We walked
through the numbers and, out of excitement and surprise, we
walked through them a second time, because I could hardly
believe what I saw: She was doing well. Very well. I felt sure
I had discovered something very special in Fatuma. If her
bookkeeping was accurate, I had before me all the makings
of a rags-to-riches story, and I imagined her going even

further. . . . Who knew how large she could grow her enterprise, if she had already done so well with just a $100 grant? (Her grant was from Village Enterprise, and I met Fatuma way back at the beginning of my journey in the spring of 2004.)

Fatuma excused herself to make tea for us. I eagerly scanned the standard-of-living questionnaire on my lap, looking for where I'd left off, so as soon as Fatuma returned I could dive back into the interview. Ah, yes. Now that we had discussed her business's revenue and costs, naturally, I wanted to hear more about what she'd done with the profits from her business. That was the whole point of her—not to mention Village Enterprise's—work, wasn't it? To empower people to create and grow their enterprises so those enterprises could provide sustainable livelihoods and a better future for people like Fatuma and others in her household.

I had seen enough by that time to know that entrepreneurs who had had as much success as Fatuma would probably have a long list of standard-of-living improvements to share with me. In anti-cipation, I turned the questionnaire on my lap over to the side of the page that was blank, so I'd have enough room to write down what I guessed would be Fatuma's lengthy list.

While Fatuma continued to prepare our tea, I scanned her simple, single-room mud home. I looked around for clues as to how she had already begun to use her profits. I saw nothing of note, no new bicycle stashed in the corner, no mosquito nets, not much of anything. I glanced outside as well. No telltale signs of newfound wealth.

Fatuma walked back into the room with our tea. I studied her. Old, worn clothing. Shoes with broken straps. I was stumped.

After the tea was poured and she was seated again across from me, I finally asked Fatuma outright how she had used the profits from her business and what her dreams were for the future. Fatuma got up from the wooden chair where she sat, glanced around, and then silently walked over to one side of the room, next to a worn mattress. She crouched low to the earth and said to me, in a low voice: "It is here." She pointed to the dirt floor with her hand. She waited for a response, but I didn't understand.

"You see, I put it . . ." After a dramatic pause, looking up at me, she continued, "in the WORLD BANK!" And with that, she laughed and laughed. So did I. She seemed to think the joke needed repeating. "You see, the World Bank! My bank!" I had to hand it to her; it was funny.

And then, after our laughter died down and she was back in her chair, I asked her again. No, really, how had she spent the profits from her businesses? She pointed back to the spot on the floor next to her mattress.

Despite her clever joke, her answer had been completely serious. She had literally buried the money in the earthen floor.

But Fatuma, I asked, have you not spent *any* of it? Why not? I needed to know. She ate three meals a day and had clothes on her body, but beyond this she lacked so many basics. Didn't she want to buy things that might improve her life? A toothbrush? A blanket? A lantern? New shoes that weren't worn through? Heck, with as much as she had earned, how about a cell phone? A motorbike?

I listed off these and several other items. Fatuma seemed only remotely interested—certainly not interested enough to dig up her money and go into town to get them anytime soon. "No, I am fine." She told me she felt better knowing that her life savings was right there, safely in the ground next to her bed. "I like having my money here," she told me.

What about growing her business activities? She could finance faster growth if she wanted to. She answered, "No, it is fine like it is."

Was she saving it for the future? Perhaps for one huge purchase? "Maybe, but I don't know."

Didn't she want her life to be better? What were her hopes? Her aspirations for her future? Her dreams for her life? "Who knows?"

she replied without much emotion. "I have no plan. I will be here. My days will pass and it is okay."

I admire people who can be content with what they have. The last thing I would want for Fatuma would be to cause her to worry and want, or to awaken some inner materialist consumer. But I felt conflicted. While I had learned by then not to prescribe a set of life improvements to anyone, I felt a responsibility to expose Fatuma to some options, especially health-related ones, that she might not have thought about before. I continued to rattle off different ideas. None of them captured her interest.

I was baffled. Up until that point in my life, every entrepreneur I had met dreamed of a better life—usually a much better life. They dreamed of booming businesses, of homes without leaky thatched roofs, of vast fields, of fattened flocks, of strong children, of educated daughters, of frequent feasts, of health and healing, of beautiful clothes, of travels to faraway places, of fast vehicles, of shiny electronics, and on and on and on. I had never encountered, not until that day, a person who seemed to have no dreams for her future.

But Fatuma could not articulate any. She did not want her life to change, and yet she did not seem to be the happiest person I'd met either. Somewhere along the way she had accepted a particular narrative for her life: that this was it. Even managing a successful microenterprise had not, apparently, changed her mind about this. She had no interest in things getting better, at least not enough to risk losing the feeling of security she may have felt sleeping next to buried treasure.

I did not keep in touch with Fatuma, so I don't know what she did with the information I gave her, or with my suggestions for ways she could improve her health or her comfort. But I think about her. I think of her quite a lot, actually. I wonder what it was that stopped her from dreaming. Was it fear? Was it a lack of courage? Or was it the thing that comes before courage—desire? If

Fatuma desired nothing more for herself, she risked nothing by her complacency. There was nothing to be courageous for. She had all she wanted: the same life she had always had. And now she had some money in the ground too. If she yearned for nothing beyond this, there was no possibility of disappointment.

I want to believe that somewhere inside, Fatuma did want something more. I hope that, somehow, since I met her a decade ago, she has tapped into those desires and has chosen to pursue them. I hope she keeps pushing forward, and does not hold back out of fear. I hope she has learned to dream, and chooses to go after those dreams. I hope she takes a bet on a better future for herself.

CHAPTER 14

Hope Is a Road

Invest Your Days

Though I admire Fatuma for many reasons, her story serves as a sobering reminder more than as a source of inspiration for me. Objectively speaking, she had achieved success with her venture and had gained relative financial wealth, but she chose to remain living the same kind of life she had always lived.

She did not use what she had to grow.

Fatuma seemed to value, over all else, the feeling of security that her savings brought her. She had lived hand to mouth her entire life before this, so it makes sense that she'd want to have an emergency fund for rainy days. She wanted to have a cushion to fall back on in case disaster struck. But the funds she had buried were much more than a cushion, and she had no plans to use them. She was simply letting her money pile up, and waiting. For what? She didn't know.

My definition of poverty has changed over time. I used to believe it was only about a lack of material needs: food, water, clothing, shelter. I thought that wealth, the opposite of poverty, was having these things. I know now that this is only a small part of the story. We are all rich in some ways and poor in others. Some people are surrounded by abundance but cannot recognize it. They are capable of great things and free to do whatever they want with their days, but they remain fearful or indecisive. They are free but feel trapped. Poverty is not just about a lack of possessions; it is, among other things, also about the belief that we cannot or should not use what we have to grow.

We all possess lessons and resources and ideas. We all have unspoken dreams hidden away in our hearts. We may even have tangible resources as well, locked away, kept out of reach, saved up, or even buried in the earth. We can keep them there. Or we can dig them up and use what we have to take risks and grow. We can constantly push ourselves to reinvest and keep flourishing.

What is the most universal, precious, inflexible asset we all possess? Time. We do not all get the same number of days on this earth, but we do all get the same number of hours in the day. We can use the time we have more courageously. Of all the resources we can use to move forward in life, how we use our time matters most.

Perhaps you've heard other advice about how to use time more efficiently, more effectively, more productively, or how to learn to multitask better. All of these things are fine, but at the end of the day (literally) what matters most is whether or not you are willing to take a bet on yourself—a bet on your wildest dreams—with an investment of your time.

What do you believe is the most valuable way you can spend your precious time? What do you consider a waste of time? Your days should reflect your answers to these questions. When they don't, it is probably because you are afraid to give up the lesser, and less risky, investments you've made.

These lesser investments do give us something in return, whether it's a steady paycheck, a sense of security, a feeling of control over our future, or any other more predictable rewards. But if you yearn to pursue an entrepreneurial path to follow your dreams, there will come a point when you can no longer hedge your bets. Eventually, to keep growing, you will need to make a trade: You will have to swap the smaller, safer bets for a larger, less certain chance at reaching your greater goals.

Don't wish for more time. Make a choice to live more courageously. Start investing your time, and all of your resources for that matter, in what you really care about, and drop the rest. It takes a brave person to give those other things up. Become that person. Make a bet on yourself.

The Escalator Principle

People often approach my husband, Reza—a scholar, writer, entrepreneur, and educator, among other things—for career guidance. It's for good reason. He has achieved remarkable levels of success in a number of categories: he became a tenured professor in his mid-thirties, he has written several international bestselling books, he has founded two successful companies, he serves on several nonprofit boards, and he's a sought-after speaker and popular media personality. When he is asked for career advice, without hesitation he refers to what we now fondly call "the escalator principle."

Reza explains that moving forward in life can be like making progress going up a down escalator. You can walk or even jog at a pretty good pace, but you'll pretty much be at a standstill. The obvious strategy is just to increase your speed and start jogging a little faster, but this isn't sustainable. Most people burn out before they reach the top. You have to be bold. You have to make big jumps and clear a few steps at once to move up in a meaningful way. It's a little scary, but that's what really gets you ahead. Big jumps.

When Reza considers the most significant moments of his life, he identifies the times when he's taken the biggest risks. For him, making those big jumps has meant taking all sorts of different risks: relocating to a new city, leaving one job for another, starting a venture from scratch, taking out insane amounts of student loans to pursue four (yes, four) higher degrees, saying yes to opportunities that he didn't feel quite ready for, giving interviews or doing media appearances on very little notice, traveling to faraway places. Not all his bets have paid off, but many of them have. And he would not be where he is today without them. They have allowed him to surge ahead in his work, beyond what even he dreamed for himself.

As I look at my own life, the escalator principle has proven itself to be true for me too. I think about the scariest, riskiest decisions I've made—the ones that took the most courage to make—and those are the ones that paid off the most. Moving across the country without a job or a plan led me to the heart of Silicon Valley. Quitting my job at Stanford to do a project in East Africa led to the inspiration for Kiva. Leaving Kiva opened up space for me to challenge myself as I never had before and to explore my potential as an entrepreneur, beyond just one venture. Challenging the status quo for retail start-up investing and fund-raising through Pro-Founder helped change crowdfunding laws. And as I write, there is a new venture in the works. As always, it's scary at the beginning. But with each new beginning I conquer and each new risk I take head-on, it gets easier to jump. It gets easier to put myself out there. It gets easier to try.

To take a big leap, there will come a point when your feet have to leave things behind. You will have to swap the smaller, safer bets for a larger, less certain chance at reaching your greater goals. There is always a cost to growth. For Fatuma, making a jump forward in her life would mean giving up the sense of safety that a stash of money gave her, and perhaps the feeling of control she had finally gained over her economic well-being. For someone else it might be a cost of time, a financial expense, an emotional vulnerability, a reputational risk, or something else.

If you yearn to pursue an entrepreneurial path to follow your dreams, there will come a point when you can no longer hedge your bets. Eventually, to keep growing, you will need to make a trade: You will have to swap the smaller, safer bets for a larger, less certain chance at reaching your greater goals. Unearth your coins. Invest everything you've got—your precious time, your unique talents, your valuable treasures—in what you care about most in this world. Make a big bet on yourself and your dreams. Right now.

Cut Out

A few years ago, I flew to Miami for a big semiannual meeting and con-ference, as my involvement with the large microfinance organization hosting the gathering mandated. As I entered the Four Seasons Hotel where the gathering was held, a blast of air conditioning instantly made my body convulse in shivers and my teeth chatter. I clenched my jaw and tried to force a smile as the concierge welcomed me.

I followed the shiny, laminated signs with cursive scrolls and gloved-hand icons pointing the way to our meeting, meandering through the wide hallways. The sound of live piano music and laughter got louder as I pulled my carry-on luggage behind me, its wheels silently carving two little lines into the plush carpet. I chuckled to myself; inside the luggage were clothes for Miami weather, but now I wished I had brought along gloves (and a hat, and a jacket, and a scarf), knowing I had to spend the next few days sitting inside one of these frigid, windowless conference rooms. I turned a corner and saw my group through the open double doors of a lavishly decorated ballroom.

Men in pastel-colored polo shirts and pleated khakis mingled with women in skirts and sundresses that could have come straight from a commercial for "island wear" ensembles. Most were gently tanned or pink-skinned from long days of golf or tennis or an afternoon sitting by the pool. Nearly all held ice-cold cocktails or glasses of wine in their manicured hands. These were familiar faces to me: some fellow board members, some staff of the organization, and some high-net-worth do-nors to the organization's work. All were crucial contributors to the organization, and as I scanned the room I realized those present were probably responsible for generously funding the majority of the year's operating expenses. I was the anomaly, a contributor of time more than money, younger and less experienced by decades, uncomfortable and unused to chic hotel ballrooms. But in addition to the goal of bringing folks together to conduct effective board meetings, these gatherings were carefully crafted to tell a particular story to attendees, one of need and of opportunity that would culminate in a series of invitations to the people in this room to become the heroes of the story by giving generously.

No one had seen me yet. Despite my genuine love for the individuals in that room, I was tired, cold, and thirsty. I scanned the edges of the crowd for a fast way through so I could grab a drink at the bar before diving into conversations with everyone. I spotted an opening and seized my opportunity, briskly making a beeline to the bar. A few seconds later I reached the long table of sparkling, stacked glassware and grabbed a glass of red. I breathed a sigh of relief and turned to face the group, looking at the crowd of friendly faces.

But what caught my eye first was an unfamiliar, dark-skinned face. It stared at me, unblinking, from the other side of the ballroom.

In fact there were several unfamiliar faces, all stationed evenly around the ballroom. All of them seemed turned in my direction, with eyes that stared right into mine and fixed smiles that seemed to remain in place, though not without effort. I blinked, not completely sure what I was seeing. I stood on tiptoe and craned my neck so I could get a better look at one of the strangers with whom a handful of people were posing for a photo. As I did, his face reflected a flash of light from the photographer's camera, and I understood. I sighed and gulped my wine.

Along the perimeter of the room were life-sized cardboard cutouts of entrepreneurs, each one representing a different country served by a microfinance institution in the portfolio, and each representing a different kind of business activity. Some of the cardboard people stood among props and equipment. In one corner was a cutout of an older woman from East Africa, smiling, holding chickens. On a rustic-looking table next to her, someone had placed a brown basket with a carton of plastic eggs alongside a plush stuffed rooster. A cutout of a younger, dark-skinned woman in a secondhand T-shirt and long skirt held some kind of grain in her hands and stood among several potted plants. On the ground beside the plants were heavy sacks of rice from a local grocery store. A cutout of another woman, mid-laugh, holding tomatoes and onions, stood behind some wooden crates filled with fake painted foam fruit and vegetables. A cutout of a middle-aged man from somewhere in South America, barefoot in rolled-up pants, leaned against one of the walls near the half-dozen light switches for the chandeliers above. Mercifully, he had no props.

I turned my gaze away from the cardboard cutouts and walked into the crowd, to talk to the living, breathing, real live pastel-clad people around me, all of whom were there to serve the kinds of entrepreneurs whose life-sized images encircled us.

It has been a very long time since I first learned about poverty, sitting on a linoleum floor in Sunday school class. Sadly, some of the stories about people living in poverty—and the thinking that motivates those stories—have not changed much. I try to filter the good from the bad, the factual from the manipulative, the realistic from the overly dramatic. Still, once in a while they get to me (like when I'm surrounded by clichéd cardboard cutouts that are supposed to make me feel closer to real people, when in fact they do the opposite), and I feel pangs of the confusion and anxiety that I did back then, as a little kid who was told that poverty could never be fixed. Once in a while I still feel overwhelmed, and the great rift between the people I want to serve and myself seems vast, no matter what I do. There are still moments when the magnitude of the problems plaguing so many people living on this planet feels crushing.

But I have learned how to fight back. I know now never to turn away from the issues that scare me. I have learned not to conflate difficult issues with the people they affect. I have learned to ask hard questions, and to get answers for myself firsthand. I know now that it is always worth getting closer to the people I want to understand, so I can hear their truths from them directly. I know not to wait for permission to explore or learn or do the things I'm passionate about. While my efforts are never perfect, I have learned that it is always worth it to keep trying.

Most important, I have become absolutely convinced that real, positive change is possible. Poverty does not have to win in the end. And anyone who *wants* to participate in making the world better *can*. Even the most "unqualified" individuals can contribute great things; even the most humble efforts can end up improving the lives of thousands or millions of people. I know without a doubt that this is true: Despite everything, we can serve each other in ways that have a permanent, lasting impact.

Our Path Forward

> *"Hope is like a road in the country; there was never a road, but when many people walk on it, the road comes into existence."*
>
> LIN YUTANG, Chinese writer and inventor

Our future is a collaborative, coauthored one. It is shared. We depend on each other. We can choose to limit ourselves, and to limit each other; or we can choose to believe that there is nothing we cannot accomplish together.

We gain the most by believing the best of one another. By telling stories about our own lives, and each others' lives, we remind ourselves that we are capable of truly great things. Our collective ability to do this—to walk alongside each other in hope—will pave our future.

Individually, what matters most in creating this future is that we each believe in our own potential to live more entrepreneurially. By that I mean to live courageously. To pursue opportunity and possibility where others see none. To enact positive change for the world in the ways that we believe in most. Collectively, what matters most is that we honor, encourage, respect, and support one another in those journeys. We must expect great things from one another. We must insist on hope.

Choose not to focus on the lack, the hurt, the poverty, or the brokenness that we all know exists. Choose to see potential and possibility. Choose to see opportunity. Choose to see strength. Choose to see strong, smart, hardworking entrepreneurs, even in unexpected places. Katherine, Blessing, Samuel, Raj, Li, and others in this book are among them. There are of course countless others. Some are right around you, running local small businesses, building start-ups, or simply working creatively at their given trade. Perhaps you are one yourself. Look for them. Learn from them. Cheer them on. Support them however you can.

And most important, let them inspire you. It is Patrick, the brick-maker, whose story nudges me to jump in and begin something new when I am feeling hesitant. It is Constance, the banana farmer, whose story challenges me to stay true to who I want to be in the world. Shona, the wheelchair builder, motivates me to look for little ways to improve, each and every day. Samuel, the goatherd, inspires me to see the extraor-dinary in ordinary places. Fatuma, the charcoal seller, reminds me to keep dreaming, and never settle for anything less. Zica, the hairdresser, reassures me that I'm ready for anything—and Leila, of course, reminds me to get up and dance.

I aspire to live my life like these entrepreneurs. They are my role mod-els for how to think, how to work, how to see the world, and how to be-lieve in myself. They refused to be held back by what they didn't have, or by what they didn't know, or by what they couldn't control. They knew that their success as entrepreneurs hinged not on what they had but on which actions they decided to take along the way in their journeys. Once again, I believe they knew inherently that, in Stevenson's words, "entre-preneurship is the pursuit of opportunity without regard to resources currently controlled." They focused on their abilities to move forward despite whatever disadvantages, risks, or barriers stood in their way.

Knowing them, and so many others like them, has been one of the greatest gifts of my life. They convinced me that I can live an entrepre-neurial life, and that I can always choose action instead of being para-lyzed by whatever barrier stands before me. It is a choice I try to make daily. It requires constant reinterpretation, and constant reinvention, as ventures and seasons of life come and go. Living an entrepreneurial life at all stages is not easy. But this is the path that I believe will help me reach my fullest potential.

What will your story be? What do you choose to see when you look at the set of possibilities for your life? Will you focus on what you don't have? Or will you choose to take action?

Please choose the courageous path. Choose to live entrepreneurially, and to take a bet on yourself. Choose to focus your precious time, talents, and energy on the pursuit of your greatest dreams. Choose to hope for more for yourself and for those around you. Dream—and then choose to believe in your own potential and help create the future you're dreaming of.

The world needs you.

A NOTE TO READERS

Over the last fifteen years, I have had the pleasure of meeting hundreds of entrepreneurs around the world. Those I've chosen to feature in this book were selected to represent some of the diversity I have observed in terms of geography, trade, sophistication, level of education, gender, age, standard of living, and so much else.

Some entrepreneurs are portrayed exactly as themselves. They have been recently and thoroughly researched for this book and for other purposes; for example, Shona McDonald and the founders of Beleza Natural were subjects of my research for a case study written under the supervision of Dean Garth Saloner at the Stanford Graduate School of Business. My work for Stanford was funded by a grant from Goldman Sachs's 10,000 Women initiative, focused on business and management education for underserved female entrepreneurs in developing and emerging markets. Shona's and the other cases I wrote during this time are extensive, much more so than what's included in this book, and publicly available to anyone who would like to learn more. For several others, including all entrepreneurs affiliated with Kiva, I changed their names and altered identifying details about them out of respect for their privacy.

Lastly, some stories, like Samuel's, Raj's, and several others, are re-called only from memory. I have cherished the interactions I've had throughout my travels where no notebook or camera has gotten in the way of the connection I'm trying to make at that moment; in fact, some of these conversations have been the most open, unhindered, genuine interactions I've had.

ACKNOWLEDGMENTS

I would like to express my gratitude to the many individuals who supported me throughout the process of writing this book by providing encouragement, feedback, edits, sanity checks, permission to include their stories or quotes, and in every other way assisted in making this book happen. I could not have done this alone.

Above all, thank you to my husband, Reza, the best book-writing guide anyone could have. You reassured, inspired, and encouraged me every day, and made me believe—through your own example—that writing something that matters to the world was within reach. You saw what this book could be even before I did; you took on the lion's share of holding down the fort at home on the many days and weekends when I had to meet deadlines; you patiently taught me whatever I needed to know at each step of the writing process; you read and reread and painstakingly edited this book in its entirety more times than I can count; you insisted on my telling the most honest story possible at every moment; you helped me find my best voice. I couldn't have asked for a better partner in this process—or in the rest of life. Thank you, my love.

Thank you, Mom and Dad, for loving every word of every version of this book (because you aren't biased at all). You have encouraged me to write for as long as I can remember, and you have been by my side at every step of my journey—even/especially the toughest steps, as I've struggled uphill or lost my footing downhill. Thank you for showing me unconditional love. Adam and Katie, thank you for also reading this book a million times already, and for being by my side every step of my life. I love you.

Thank you, Marly Rusoff, for believing in the potential for the book when it was just an idea. Thank you to Celina Spiegel and Julie Grau for taking a bet on me and publishing this book, to Jessica Sindler for her insightful edits, and to the entire Spiegel and Grau team for believing in this project and in me.

Thank you to the faculty, staff, and administrative family at the Stanford Graduate School of Business. Thank you, Julie Juergens, for hiring me into the GSB family, where my eyes were opened to the power of entrepreneurship to change the world. Thank you to Peggy Reid for coaching me, mentoring me, and being such a good friend through so many ups and downs. Thank you to Dr. Yunus, whose talk in the fall of 2003 changed the trajectory of my life. Jim Patell, thank you for teaching me that professionals take it personally, and for not hesitating to answer "Get out of here! Go to Africa!" when I sought your advice on whether or not to take that big leap in the spring of 2004, and for teaching me that almost anything can be fixed if you have a good pocket knife and some duct tape. Jennifer Aaker, you are a friend and mentor to me like no one else in my life. Thank you for the steady encouragement throughout the years. Thank you, Garth Saloner, for allowing me to spend a year being inspired by some of the most amazing entrepreneurs in the world, at a time when (whether you knew it or not) that was exactly what I needed to be reinspired in my own entrepreneurial journey. Thank you, Derrick Bolton, for not accepting me the first time around (really!) and for accepting me into the class of 2007; the timing was perfect.

Thank you to all of those who believed in me and in the idea of Kiva from the beginning. Brian Lehnen, you gave me my first "big break," and put yourself and your organization on the line to help Kiva get up and running from day one. You have been the best of mentors and friends ever since we met. Thank you. Bob and Dottie King, thank you for the very early advice and encouragement on long, bumpy rides in big white safari vans throughout East Africa (and back home too), and for treating me like family ever since.

Thank you to the earliest Kiva supporters and team members. Thank you to our first board members, especially Reid Hoffman, Alex Edelstein, Tabreez Verjee, Leslie Crutchfield, and Geoff Davis, for nurturing Kiva in its infancy. Thank you to Julie Hanna, John D. Muller, Amy Klement, and other board members who have joined since, who have contributed so much to the organization's success. Premal, thank you for our one-of-a-kind friendship, and for leading Kiva as only you could through thick and thin. And Matt, thank you for changing the course of my whole life. Before it was anything else, Kiva was our journey, and I am grateful for every step of it.

To my dearest of friends: Thank you to the entire ProFounder family—Dana Mauriello, Ryan Garver, Olana Khan, David Lang, Rachel Tobias, Adam Anderson, Sathya Sekaran, and Kate Karas—for an extraordinary journey together, and thank you to our earliest advisors and investors for making the journey possible.

Shannon, you have been there for me through thick and thin and are the truest of true friends. Knowing you is one of the greatest gifts in my life. Chelsa, thank you for your deep and faithful friendship. Of all the wonderful things that have come to me in life because of Kiva, having met you is the very best one. You have always lifted me up when I needed it most and encouraged me to be my best self—and all the other times in between. Olana and Zain, you have loved, supported, and believed in me, and even given me a home for so many months. Dennis and Stacey Barsema, thank you for giving me a place to live, write, heal, and dream when I needed it most, and for being so supportive of me throughout the years. I am grateful!

And last but so important, thank you to all of the entrepreneurs in this book, and the countless others around the world who have inspired and fueled me. I hope I have told your stories in the way you would have wanted.

ABOUT THE TYPE

This book was set in Minion, a 1990 Adobe Orig-
inals typeface by Robert Slimbach. Minion is inspired by classical, old-style typefaces of the late
Renaissance, a period of elegant and beautiful
type designs. Created primarily for text setting,
Minion combines the aesthetic and functional
qualities that make text type highly readable with
the versatility of digital technology.